UNDATEABLE

311 Things Guys Do That Guarantee They Won't Be Dating or Having Sex

Ellen Rakieten and Anne Coyle

Villard New York

A Villard Books Trade Paperback Original

Published in the United States by Villard Books, an imprint of The Random House Publishing Group, a division of Random House, Inc., New York.

VILLARD BOOKS and VILLARD & "V" CIRCLED Design are registered trademarks of Random House, Inc.

Library of Congress Cataloging-in-Publication Data

Rakieten, Ellen.
Undateable : 311 things guys do that guarantee they won't be dating or having sex / Ellen Rakieten and Anne Coyle.
        p. cm.
"A Villard Books trade paperback original."
ISBN 978-0-345-52067-8 (pbk.)
1. Men—Humor. 2. Dating (Social customs)—Humor. 3. Man-woman relationships—Humor. I. Coyle, Anne. II. Title.
PN6231.M45R35 2010
818'.602—dc22
2009045859

Printed in the United States of America
www.villard.com
9 8 7 6 5 4 3 2 1

Design and creative direction: Tereasa Surratt/The Royal Order of Experience Design, Chicago

Photos provided by Ryan Baehr, Kaitlyn Webster, Joris de Vrede, guidofistpump.com, and American Spirit Images/Unlisted Images, Inc.

Anne Coyle author photograph courtesy of Eric Hausman
Ellen Rakieten author photograph courtesy of William Waldron

Elaine: "So basically what you're saying is ninety-five percent of the population is undateable?"

Jerry: *"Undateable!"*

Elaine: "So how are all these people getting together?"

Jerry: *"Alcohol."*

Seinfeld
"The Wink"
October 1995

Dedications

To P.B.K., the most Dateable man I know. To Zack and Nicky, lovable, huggable, future Dateables. Life without you UNLIVABLE. To all the women who shared their Undateables with us...he's out there, sometimes they just need a little help... To all the guys who can easily go from Undateable to Dateable if you follow our advice: We really DO LOVE you all—just don't say "Booya!"

X Elle

To Bill and Charlie, my two favorite people on the planet. I love you beyond. Rawr. To my parents, for their unfailing kindness and unflinching moral compass. Thank you for being the parents who understood that Monty Python was not the devil's work. To Mickey, Scott, and Luke. The older I get, the funnier it was. To Elles Belles...my other sister and a girl I love so much my ex-husband still thinks we're involved. Thank you for your life-enhancing magic. Neighbors for life. xo.

XO Anne

Acknowledgments

Special love to those who helped with this book, those who helped shape my life, and those I count on every day...Oprah (like my mom said, "you had me longer than she did," eternal ♥ ellie bellie). Jessica and Jerry S (my "cup of tea," sugar and honey!). Adam Glassman (so Dateable it's crazy!). Jorgie Porgie (forever and a day!). Ali Cat (your Undateables are all sexual, hmmm?). The extraordinary Meghan "Bee" Hoffman (have you signed your lifelong contract yet?). Jen A & Kristin Hahn (I treasure our "girls only" date nights). Michael C (it's 10:00 p.m.— meet you on our bench!). Tom Papa (thanks for the toenail joke!). Team CAA— Steve L, Alix H, Tony E, Alan B, Rosi B... led by the incomparABLE Kevin Huvane. Jeanne Newman (my North Star!). Benny Medina (for holding up the mirror). Kenny Paves (nothing I wouldn't do for you!). Jillian Michaels & GC Chersich (we were meant to be!). Our brilliant literary agent, Andrea Barzvi (we're so into you!). Our devoted editor, Jennifer Smith, and visionary publisher, Jane von Mehren, and publicity gurus Theresa Zoro and Sharon Propson, plus the entire Random House crew—fantastic! The Royal Order for understanding that Steve McQueen is the ultimate Dateable. Heidi Krupp (you're one bad-ass superstar!). Bob Miller (so grateful!). Jan Miller (you're a force of nature!). Amy Duffy (the daughter I always wanted!). Lindsey Kotler (the little sister I finally got!). Seth Marks, Shawn Wilson, Craig Robinson, Michael Hainey, Stedman Graham, Billy Bush, and Mark Consuelos (you could teach the ultimate "get Dateable" class!).

My cherished Harpo family—there are SO many of you that naming all would take up the whole book...Sher, Lisa E, Howie, Jonny Sinc, Layla, Jillie Jill V, Jill B, Lisa H, Lisa M, Katy, Lesia, Sally Lou, Amy & Neil, Gina, Jen S, Siobhan, Megan S, Cindy M, Gayle K...and on and on and on...

Annie Cabannie/AC399/Slimmy...You are my beloved long-legged golden girl. From the first moment I saw you in that sick gray coat I knew it was love and a little bit of lust. You fill in all my blanks. Long live the 8th floor! xo er

As always, I want to express my infinite love to my parents, Marilyn and Stanley, my sister, Nancy, my brother, Steven, and my mother-in-law, Barbara...luckiest girl in the world I am.

– E.R.

Thanks to many superbly talented and supportive people. Tereasa Surratt for designing a kick-ass proposal. Dave Hernandez, for marrying Tereasa. Tim, Kyle, and David at the Royal Order, for their creative genius, humor, and total dateability. To Ryan Baehr, photographer extraordinaire. Thank you for the perfect photographs. Meghan Hoffman, for your dedication and your diligence. And for laughing at everything I say. Lisa Carron, for your kindness and commitment, but most of all for your supremely special brain. To P.B.K., the 8th-floor husband and a true friend. E.S., thanks for turning on the lights. To C.H. for really being there. A.M. and B.H.M. for loving this idea (and me). And S.B., a total rockstar.

– A.C.

Contents

WTF?

WAS IT SOMETHING I DID?

WAS IT SOMETHING

I SAID? WAS IT

SOMETHING I WORE?

YES, YES, AND YES.

We've all heard the story a million times. A nice single girl has been hearing about this guy for weeks. "He's a great guy! He's fun! He's smart and really well read. He's not George Clooney, but he's cute. My brother loves him!"

The guy calls the girl, and they arrange to meet for dinner. He has a nice voice and she's feeling really good about this one. As she waits for him at the bar, she allows herself to fantasize that this might be the day that she will remember as "the moment," the moment he walked in and she knew he was the one...

And then he walks in. Sporting hair plugs. Hey, that's okay, she thinks. I'm a person of depth. I mean, I'm not really a fan, but maybe once we start talking I can move beyond it...

Or not. Somewhere between the unending sports metaphors ("Let's say we move the ball forward and get a table!") and the reveal of a large black cell phone strapped to his pleated Dockers, things are not looking good. After he orders his second Long Island Iced Tea, she realizes the only thing that could pull her out of this

1

death spiral is his confessing that he is in fact a French count impersonating a complete loser as an assignment for an acting class.

But no, that doesn't happen. This happens...the Mother of All Undateables. He pushes back his chair, stands up, and without a moment of hesitation, out it comes: "I'll be back. I gotta take a dump."

Date...OVER. Relationship?...NOT. Guy?...UNDATEABLE.

Let's face it. Women are complicated creatures, and at times hard to understand. But the reality is, there's an unspoken list of things men say, wear, or do that will pretty much guarantee that the girl you just took out to dinner won't ever want to see you again. Or if she does, it will be to tell you that she "just wants to be friends." These are the mistakes that render men UNDATEABLE. And the sad part is, you guys usually don't have a clue what happened.

We know you've been there. There's this fantastic girl you like. She's pretty, funny, smart, and caring. She's single. She's friendly. But you can't crack the code. You ask yourself...WTF? What's going on here? Was it something I said? *(YES!)* Was it something I did? *(YES!)* Was it something I wore? *(YES! YES! YES!)*

We interviewed hundreds of smart, funny, normal women from all walks of life and asked them for their lists of Undateables, the things that turned a guy from a MAYBE into a NO WAY. Some answers were more obvious (readjusting the "family jewels" over drinks), while others were randomly brilliant (owning a cat), and some we never saw coming (using the phrase "my lover.").

Now, for the first time, we're giving you the never-before-revealed "list," a brutally honest collection of the things men do to turn women off. The book is broken down into three main parts: What Not to Wear, What Not to Say, and What Not to Do. In these chapters, we will be listing, in excruciating written and visual detail, the actual mistakes made by millions of men that stop them from romantically connecting with women.

These mistakes will also be rated, from the fairly innocent to the completely hideous, and an icon to indicate the seriousness of the offense will accompany each rating level.

Perhaps, after reading the first few pages, you'll think we're just a bunch of uptight, judgmental nightmares. And maybe we are. But make no mistake...we love men. And because we love you, we need to tell you the truth. We need to tell you what all those women who aren't returning your calls or who "just want to be friends" don't have the heart to tell you themselves.

FOR ANY GUY WHO'S EVER WONDERED, "WHAT DID I DO?" HERE'S WHAT YOU DID...

RATING SYSTEM

In presenting the list of Undateables, we've included a rating system. There's a large range in the severity of the transgressions we've collected. Some mistakes are minor...they might set you back for a few minutes, but you CAN recover. Then there are the mistakes that have women literally making a run for it...

Red Flag

Storm Cloud

**Not
Getting Any**

Kiss of Death

These are innocent mistakes, but mistakes nonetheless. These foibles can usually be corrected by a trip to a clothing store or a rethink on the vocabulary. You're still in the game, but you have alerted her to the fact that you are not flawless. See "Booya!," #119. And Tube Socks, #44.

Either your abundance of red flags or a more serious offense has created a general sense of unease and concern. Like storm clouds on the horizon, your issues indicate a much more grave problem. The storm cloud puts a woman on alert. These are hard to overcome, but it is possible. You have about five minutes to turn it around. See Jeans While Skiing, #8.

Major issue. Something that makes a woman say or think, *Ewww* or *Gross*. You are now officially NOT SEXY. AT ALL. Probably best to pack it in here. Your only hope is to let a few weeks pass, and then call to explain that Walgreens completely gave you the wrong medication, and that's why you said, "How 'bout we go Dutch this time. It's kinda pricey!" *Husbands/boyfriends take note: If you are seriously dating or married, a minor red flag can often land you here. It's not fair, but it's a fact. Unfortunately, the longer you've been together, the less serious the transgression has to be to render you unsexable. Unjust...but true.*

We're done here. You're a freak. Mistakes of this magnitude typically result in the girl leaving the date "with stomach problems" or an incoming phone call alerting her to a family emergency that she needs to attend to *RIGHT NOW*. See Speedos, #53.

But wait...
help is on the way.

You didn't think we were going to point out the error
of your ways and then leave you in the dust, did you?
Because we're nice (and love a good makeover), we're
going to help you right the wrongs. Some mistakes
are unfixable (see Skullet, #97), while others can be
corrected with some really good advice and a credit
card (see Hawaiian Shirts, #30). Whenever you see
the Red Cross, that means we are offering you help...a
failproof solution to your issue and a big step on your
way to becoming Dateable again.

A Few Notes on How to Read This Book...

If you're under twenty-one:
The subtitle of the book is *311 Things Guys Do to Guarantee They Won't Be Dating or Having Sex*. The key word here is "guys," and by "guys" we mean someone over the age of twenty-one. (Any younger and you're still considered a boy.) By the time you're twenty-one, you are working (hopefully) and beginning to make your way in the world. That's the time to start pulling it together in terms of how you're presenting yourself. Up until then, you're still learning, and this is the time to make mistakes, try some stuff out, and see if it works for you. So wear a porkpie hat, have a lightsaber fight, order a Tom Collins, and say, "That's what I'm talking about" at will. And if you read this book and feel there's something in here that makes sense, great. But don't take it too seriously. Because part of the fun of growing up is wearing ridiculous clothes, saying stupid phrases, and doing idiotic things. And then laughing about it later.

A word about swagger:
There may be a few of you who read this book and think, *Who the hell do these women think they are, telling us what to wear, what to say, and how to act? I'll do whatever the f*** I want.* To that we say, GOOD FOR YOU. Seriously. As one of our guy friends said, "Everyone's got the right to develop their own swagger." And we couldn't agree more. If you love your bowling shirts and think your pinkie rings are hot, then keep wearing them and tell us to go jam it. Because in the end, what women really love is a guy who knows what he likes and has the balls to stick to it. So guys, listen closely, because this is what you really need to know: **THERE IS NOTHING SEXIER THAN A MAN WITH CONFIDENCE.**

And with that said...

WHAT
NOT TO
WEAR

That'sHot

The good news here is that many of these things are fixable. The bad news is that once a woman sees you in any of these getups, you have been compromised.

Depending on the transgression, you may be able to pull it out, but you're going to have to do something pretty spectacular to turn this into a Cinderella story. It's unfortunate, because she'll never know that you teach small children and love Lenny Kravitz. All she knows is that you're wearing a Holiday Sweater.

Note: a lot of these are RED FLAGS, which are the most innocent of Undateables. And honestly, there is something to be said for a guy who isn't overly coiffed and fashion-savvy. (That's a whole different Undateable.) Plus, what woman doesn't love a good makeover?

Jorts:
just say no.

1. JORTS In case you're confused, the "jort" is a cross between a pair of jeans and a pair of shorts. They are essentially jean shorts, hitting the victim's leg somewhere between the upper thigh and the calf. Perhaps the most ill-conceived item of male clothing ever invented, they come in a wide variety of styles and lengths, all of which are hideous in any circumstance. Let's put it this way…mega star Justin Timberlake can't even pull this off. And he's really rich.

> *Jorts are confusing. Do you want to wear jeans or shorts? Our guess is that what you're really saying is that you'd like to wear a longish, slouchy pair of shorts and not look too buttoned-up. You'd like to look more casual. In that case, here are your options: Flat-front cotton khaki shorts hitting somewhere in the range of your knee. No shorter. (Short shorts are their own special problem. See Flood Shorts, #89.) A classic cargo short; these can be a smidge longer, just at the bottom of the knee. Steer clear of the calf. (For more specific guidance, go to undateable.com.)*

Oh. My. Freaking. God. Stop it.

☠️ **2. BAD FACIAL HAIR** Handlebars. Mutton-chops. The Fu Manchu. Whatever. No commentary necessary. Let's move on.

⛈️ **3. SOUL PATCH** A.K.A. "the Dirty Chin" or "Flavor Saver." This is the bit of hair right under the lip, just above the chin. These come in different shapes, sizes, and colors. All are nasty. Once in a while, a certain type of guy can pull this off, but it's rare.

> **TRUE STORY:** *Our friend Annabelle (36) was fixed up with a really great guy. Friends with her friends, cute, good body, politically and morally aligned, divorced with kids (like her): He had great potential. But there was that hairy patch she just couldn't get past. When her friends said, "Just tell him to shave it," she thought for a minute and realized, "The problem is I can't shave off the part of his brain that thought growing it was a good idea." Really, guys, after a certain age, it just says too much about some of your bigger issues.*

Nice Brazilian.   *No.*   *Nope.*   *Hell no.*

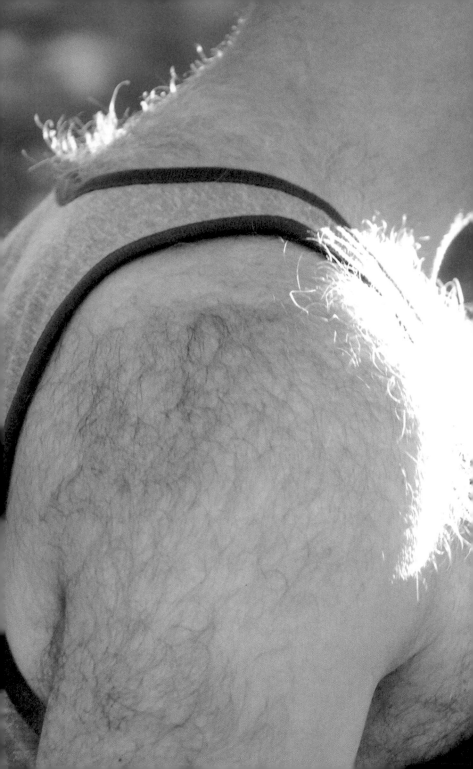

Nice sweater, Chewie.

4. HAIRY BACK, NECK, NOSE, OR EARS
Excess fur needs to be trimmed, waxed, shaved…whatever you need to do, just do it, and keep it to yourself. No one wants to hear about it.

5. HAIR PLUGS If your intention was to have women look at nothing but your hairline and visualize how searingly painful that procedure actually was, then this was a success. If it was to cover up the fact that you are losing your hair, then no, it didn't work. Not even a little.

6. UGLY GRAY SWEATPANTS Three clues why these are a big, smelly turn-off: UGLY, GRAY, and SWEATPANTS. Do what you like at home alone, but on a date? Please.

7. OVERLY COLOGNED Way to announce yourself six minutes before you actually enter the room. Yowsa. Your strong and stanky scent is burning our eyes. It's also ensuring that no matter what we order for dinner, it will taste like Drakkar Noir. You've already assaulted three of our five senses and we don't even know if you rent or own.

 Let's back it down a bit and try something a little less, um, disgusting. There are lots of lovely products out there that don't make you smell like you've been dipped in old brandy and then rolled in talcum powder. Try the more understated approach of the aftershave balm with a hint of geranium, citrus, lavender, sage, rosemary, cedarwood, or cucumber.

8. JEANS WHILE SKIING

Just so you know, there is an item of clothing called "ski pants" or "snow pants" that are made specifically for this purpose. They're waterproof and insulated to keep you warm. Get a pair.

 9. *CORPORATE SWAG* Windbreakers, sweatshirts, golf shirts, and gym bags emblazoned with the company logo scream "free clothes." Don't look to your employers to dress you. They've got other things to do, like running the company. Never in the history of human sexuality has a woman ever passionately growled, "I can't wait to get home and rip that Met Life shirt off you."

10. *TIGHTY WHITIES* Just plain creepy.

If for some reason the traditional boxers don't work for you (no need to explain), move to stretch cotton boxer briefs that touch at least a part of your thigh. But boxers are highly desirable.

sexy as a serial killer.

 11. ROLLED-UP JEANS Who are you, Sandra Dee? All you need is a pair of white slip-on sneakers and you can lie belly-down on your shag carpet and write in your diary. Don't forget to lock it!

> *A note about jeans: You really need to pay close attention here. Get the jeans wrong and your whole outfit is screwed. Jeans should be medium to dark blue, unembellished, unmarred, hang on your hips, cover your ankles, and extend to at least the top of the shoes. Levi's 501s always work. End of story.*

12. BLACK JEANS You know what looks really good with black jeans? Nothing. You know why? Because they're really ugly. Jeans should be blue. Sure, we know there are people who can work this look, but most guys can't. Unless you're a rail-thin artist or musician, please don't attempt this. You'll just end up looking like you're attending a funeral in Mississippi.

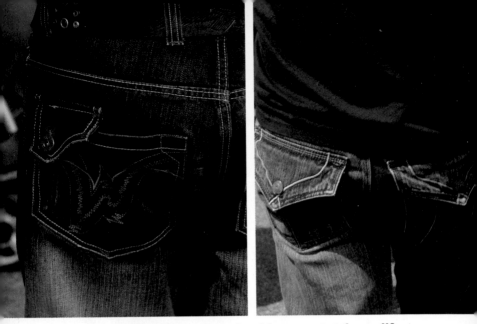

Omigod! What time should we meet at the mall?

13. EMBELLISHED JEANS Studded with rivets, designed with crystal swirls, embroidered, tattooed, painted...In your sincere attempt to be "hip," you have actually ended up dressing like a seventeen-year-old girl.

 14. DAD JEANS Waist-high jeans are never, ever flattering. They produce a phenomenon known as "long butt," rendering your behind SpongeBob SquarePants–esque. Actually, Dad Jeans are really just a version of the universally disdained Mom Jeans, but worn by a man. *Note: If you iron your jeans to create a crease down the middle or ask the dry cleaner to press your jeans, you've already introduced yourself without saying a word. You're a pain in the ass.*

15. ACID-WASHED JEANS This look should have died a natural death in the mid-1970s, but like a willful vampire it just won't stay down. Let's end this thing, shall we?

 16. PRE-RIPPED JEANS You may have noticed these shredded jeans on Rihanna and Lindsay Lohan. Fine. Great on young starlets…not on men.

 17. SKY-BLUE JEANS Not sure why, but this always says "BIG HUGE PUSSY."

Do these jeans make me look lame?

A.K.A. The Canadian Tuxedo

18. *NOVELTY BELT BUCKLES* Find another way to express yourself.

19. *THE BEN FRANKLIN (BALD ON TOP WITH HAIR ON SIDES)* Thank you so much for inventing electricity. We love it! Now go shave the rest of your head.

20. *DOUBLE DENIM* This is a denim shirt or denim jacket worn with jeans, which gives the illusion that you're wearing a denim jumpsuit. We know you love them both, but you're going to have to choose one or the other. Sorry. And don't go thinking that you can get away with substituting a "chambray" shirt for a denim one, either. They're the same thing. Plus, we're pretty sure "chambray" is French-Canadian for "douche."

21. SPORTS JERSEYS Only acceptable at a sporting event with the guys. Actually, we take that back. This whole look is just plain queer. And by queer, we don't mean gay. A gay man wouldn't be caught dead in one. They make you look like a big, lumbering seven-year-old.

> **66 99** GQ's Glenn O'Brien (A.K.A. "the Style Guy") writes, "I find the customs of jersey wearing, face painting, and carnival-like costumes to be a few of the more horrifying aspects of postmodern life. Makes one sympathize with how the Romans felt when the Huns showed up." Jay-Z, mogul: "I don't wear jerseys, I'm 30+."

22. COSBY SWEATERS The legendary "Cos" pulled it off, but back then we were all eight years old and didn't know any better. No one in the history of time has ever worn one of these and looked even remotely sexy. Or to put it another way, don one of these woollen tragedies and it's a lock that no woman will come near your pudding pop.

A.K.A. The Cosby Sweater

Weekend White Guy

You've seen these guys walking the streets of every city and suburb, dressed in their play clothes. During the week, the WWG is undercover as a normal, mature adult in a dark suit and decent shoes, doing important things at the office. But when the weekend comes, he's as clueless as they come. You can spot a WWG by his high-waisted, flood-length pleated khaki shorts, the thin black/brown belt he wears to work, white athletic socks (neatly folded), running sneakers or mandals, and a golf shirt, a Hawaiian shirt, or a variation of a Tommy Bahama top. If he's wearing the golf shirt, emblazoned on his left breast will most likely be the logo of the last resort he's been to, almost always for a company event. And to top it all off, he's typically wearing either a visor (ahhh!) or a baseball cap with yet another logo on the front. Strap on a cell phone holster and you've got Weekend White Guy. WWGs are usually easy to fix, because they really don't care about fashion. At all. They're like big dolls, ready to be dressed.

Is anything as appealing as mesh-covered nipples?

Yes! We see you.

 23. MESH CLOTHING When you wear mesh clothing, are you telling us that you're so hot, if you wore regular clothes they would burst into flames? These clothes are appropriate nowhere.

 24. PORKPIE HATS You have revealed yourself as someone who spends a lot of time putting together his "look" and posing in front of the mirror. Verbal attacks on the porkpie are usually defended with the "What? It's vintage" argument. Guess what? There are a LOT of really crappy old ideas. Overly self-aware and annoying.

 25. COLORED CONTACT LENSES Wow, this is really terrifying. You look like an alien. Wait, are you sure you're not here to puncture my ovaries and extract my life beans?

ho. ho...no.

26. HOLIDAY SWEATERS Frankly, there is just no excuse for a holiday sweater. We get that someone gave it to you as a gift...we don't care. And in terms of carrying on a "family tradition," take a few minutes and grow a pair.

how to look like a dork.

27. MANDANNAS If you truly look like Matthew McConaughey or happen to land the starring role in the next Indiana Jones movie, go for it. Otherwise, save it for the surf boys under twenty-one. Actually, scratch that. Indy is way too much of a man to ever wear a mandanna.

28. GUYLIGHTS Highlighting, frosting, or bleaching your hair. Why is it the guys with the biggest muscles do the absolute girliest things? Hmmm. Go tell your date that you'll pick her up as soon as you're done "frosting your tips" and let us know how that goes.

29. MAKEUP Big problem. Bronzer, manscara, guyliner, male polish…whatever. It's abnormal. Remember…you're a guy. A "yes" to makeup means a "no" to making out.

30. HAWAIIAN SHIRTS Here's the issue... Hawaiian shirts have made it to the mainland. They don't work anywhere and yet they are everywhere. That goes for the ubiquitous Tommy Bahama–like top as well. You've been spotted sporting these at the grocery store, out to dinner, at the airport, at work, at church, even at the company picnic. Made in hideous fabrics, these shirts scream "Insurance man letting it all hang out." You are now officially UNSEXABLE.

Cheesy-burger in paradise.

> Here's the deal...next time you reach for that Hawaiian shirt, don't. Instead, go with a polo shirt or long-sleeved, lightweight cotton oxford shirt in white, pale blue, or a mild stripe. Your best bet is to keep it untucked and un-ironed. Roll up the sleeves and off you go.

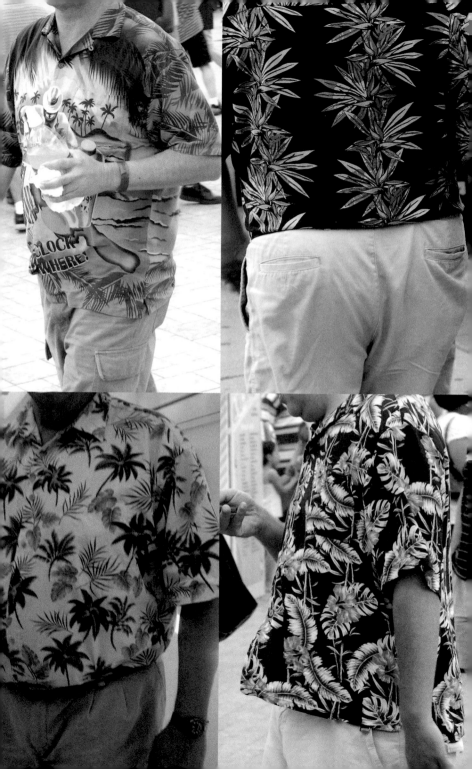

"G"

"G" is a different animal from Weekend White Guy. WWGs are basically normal people who just need some intense fashion advice and a little more social interaction. G, however, is a bit of a head case. Somewhere along the line, G's wires got crossed and now he thinks he's a black gangsta rapper. He is neither black, nor a gangsta, nor a rapper. But this doesn't stop him from sporting the baggy japris, hugely oversized T-shirts, lots of bling, a backward or sideways baseball cap, and brand-new gym shoes. G calls his friends "Playa" and "G," which is, of course, short for "gangsta." He addresses his date as "shorty" or "homegirl." G is kind of scary because he is delusional. G would need a whole team of really good doctors to fix him.

Hey, Tex, you gettin' ready for a conference-call showdown at the O.K. Corral?

31. PIMP SHOES When wearing a pair of shoes, ask yourself the following questions: "Are these shoes fly?" "Would they look good with a purple suit?" "Are they faux crocodile, alligator, or sharkskin?" "Have you ever seen anything quite like them?" If you answered yes to any of these questions, you are wearing a pair of pimp shoes.

32. CELL PHONE ON WAIST Whether you clip it on or you're packin' it in a holster, this says "Middle-management tool with a long commute." *NOTE: A clip-on anything is hideous, including a tie.*

33. LONGISH FINGERNAILS Keep your fingernails clean and short. Anything longer than a week's growth is highly suspect.

ass-inine.

☠ **34. BUSTIN' A SAG** Overly baggy pants where the waist gathers around your thighs so your underwear and your ass can hang out. (Yes, you just read that correctly.) From rappers to twelve-year-old boys, this look is ass-inine. Pull up your pants.

> " " *"If you've ever wondered where this trend started, look no further than your local county lock-up. Word is, this lovely look was originally referred to as jailin'—as it first became en vogue around the prison yard. Belts are confiscated when men go to jail, so their pants are always falling down." —Billie K.*

Just. Plain. Wrong.

 35. APRON WHILE COOKING Your pumps better match your apron or we're going to have to come in there and beat you again.

 36. MURSE A.K.A. "man purse." If you need to carry your gear, a chic briefcase, a messenger bag, or a backpack is the only acceptable option.

> **" "** *Andy Roddick is not a fan of the man purse. The tennis star has lashed out on his website against the growing English trend. Roddick writes, "I have seen some guys walking around with man purses here in London...anything bigger than a money clip or a wallet is to be left to your girlfriend/wife...and just so we are clear you should not be able to throw your 'wallet' over your shoulder."*

37. BIKE SHORTS Unless you are a serious cyclist in training or Lance Armstrong, steer clear. You'll just end up looking like the world's worst superhero.

croc-a-sh*t

38. CROCS If you're a surgeon or a short-order cook and spend a significant amount of time on a tiled or hard stone floor, these are genius. Everyone else needs to stop it. Even Facebook users have formed a group called "Crocs: I don't care how comfortable they are. You look like a dumbass." That means you potentially have 350 million people thinking this is a really bad idea.

39. TURQUOISE JEWELRY Hmmm. There are a few options here. Aging, washed-up cowboy. Pot-throwing, pot-smoking hippie. New Age, crystal-loving enlightened guy. Even though we're not a fan of the look, we admire your authenticity. The bigger problem is that guy who picks it up on the beach in Mexico or at the gift shop in Santa Fe and decides, "It's me." Let's hope not.

40. PINKIE RINGS If you're wearing a pinkie ring, let's consider what you're telling us about yourself. You feel a kinship to fur coats, pimps, Vegas, drug dealers, mobsters, silk shirts, Guidos, and Liberace. If that's what you want to tell us, okay. You just need to understand that this look is very limiting. Sex? Fuhgeddaboutit!

41. CAMOUFLAGE JACKETS Something tells us that if you show up for a date in a camo jacket, you're probably not looking for a love connection. You're more likely looking to confiscate our canned goods and smuggle them back to your makeshift bomb shelter. Very Unabomber.

42. SIDEWAYS BASEBALL HAT A.K.A. "the Hat Tilt." Unfortunately, this has become a national epidemic. The fact that you stood in front of the mirror, making your puckered-lipped "I'm so cool" face, propping your "lid" at the perfect angle to get this exact look, is so loserish it scares us. You don't look like a stud. You look like a complete tool.

> **"** *Sideways baseball hats must be stopped — what you think it says about you: I'm just one of the bros, bro! What it actually says about you: I am a hapless follower who can easily be convinced to drink my own pee."*
> *—Lemondrop.com*

 43. WHITE SOCKS WITH ANYTHING OTHER THAN ATHLETIC SHOES We believe this lecture is happening below. See our rant under Tube Socks, #44.

 44. TUBE SOCKS Only allowed on the court or on the field. We get that you can buy them in bulk, but don't. One pair is already too many.

> *If you don't even know what sort of athletic socks to wear, we sense your confusion extending to pretty much all shoe/sock combinations. Just so we're clear, for sports, you should be wearing white, calf-height athletic socks. Don't pull these up. Let them gather haphazardly about your ankles. You should only wear athletic socks with athletic shoes. If you're wearing any other sort of shoe, you need to wear plain dark socks in cotton, wool, or a blend, depending on the season. Navy blue is usually fine. (Note: Do not wear black socks unless you're wearing black dress pants or a black suit.) Also, if it's not super-cold, going sockless is excellent when wearing loafers, sneakers, white bucks, et cetera. (These shoes are to be worn with jeans, khakis, shorts, et cetera.) Sandals? Don't even think about wearing a sock with these. See "Mandal" with socks, #49.*

45. TRANSITIONS SUNGLASSES These are the glasses that get darker as the sun gets brighter. The problem is, one minute you're talking to a seemingly normal person. The next minute his glasses have gone dark and he looks like someone who's going to put a burlap sack over your head and wrestle you into his van...never to be seen again.

46. FLIP-UPS These are the "sun shades" that cover your regular glasses. We get that it's a money saver, but here are your options in terms of dealing with sun: (1) Buy a pair of real sunglasses. (2) Keep your eyes closed. (3) Stay inside.

47. BODY PIERCINGS We're all for being creative and expressing oneself. How about painting...or a photography class? Piercing the lips, tongue, nipples, nose, those giant ear expander disks...kind of disturbing. And yes, we've all heard of the heightened sexual pleasures created by the pierced tongue. Still don't care. You still have to talk to people's parents and your boss with that thing.

47.

"What you think it says about you: I am super alternative. What it actually says about you: I have made an irreparable mistake." —Lemondrop.com

That's hot.   *Sweet combo!*

 48. FANNY PACKS We get how convenient they are. But even so, there is never an excuse for a "fanny" pack. You're going to end up looking like someone's grandmother at Disneyland. If you're out there hiking, shopping, or traveling, get a backpack or a messenger bag.

 49. THE "MANDAL" WITH SOCKS As coined by Adam Glassman, creative director of *O* magazine. That would be a man sandal worn with socks. Athletic socks are ridiculous, but you jump to maximum-penalty status if you're caught wearing sandals with, dare we say, black socks.

 50. BLING There are about nine men on the planet who can pull this off. You need to know who you are, and have the profession to back it up. Rappers and sports stars can get away with it. Everybody else, remember…dogs, not diamonds, are a man's best friend.

thumbs down, bro.

51. GIRLIE SUNGLASSES Hey, have a great lunch with Beyoncé and Posh Spice. And be sure to order the Cobb…it's to die for!

52. BIG BAD BOXY POLYESTER TOPS A.K.A. "the BBBPT." Truly one of the most shocking garments on the planet. *What are these?* The only way one of these makes any sense is if (A) you were just released from the penitentiary and they gave it to you so you didn't leave nude, (B) you're a blackjack dealer from Vegas, in which case you don't care what you're wearing as long as you are outside breathing real oxygen and not surrounded by red velvet walls, (C) you're a carny who operates the Tilt-A-Whirl. That's it. The rest of you need to pull it together and start caring again. Seriously, if I were a guy, I'd rather leave the house in a muumuu than wear one of these.

the dreaded

☠ **53. *SPEEDOS*** A.K.A. "Grape Smuggler,"
"Banana Hammock." Even if you're a fit
European hottie or an Olympic swimmer,
wearing this will elicit gasps of horror from
women in any age group. Even other men will
feel the need to look away. Deal f'ing breaker.
Stay at the beach. We're going to dinner.

Anal Andy

The bummer about Andy is that he'd be
a great husband in terms of helping out.
You'd never have to do the dishes, change a
lightbulb, or sweep out the garage. He'd do the
laundry, do the shopping, and hook up your
stereo. You've met guys like Andy. "I'm Anal
Andy, at your service. I'm right here, ready
to help. All day. 24/7. By the way, did you
realize your gutters need cleaning? Anyhoo,
you can't let that go too long, or you're going
to have a frickin' mess!" SHUT UP, ANDY! The
problem with Andy is, he's a colossal pain
in the ass. After five minutes with Andy you
want to stab yourself in the eye with a pencil.
When it comes to his clothing, Andy is very
neat. Pleated-front pants or jeans are always
pressed with a crisp crease right down the
front. All shirts must have a collar and are
ironed within an inch of their life, even on
the weekends. Andy doesn't leave the house
without checking the weather, and he carries
a small collapsible umbrella and an extra
sweater or windbreaker "just in case." If
Andy is feeling good, he may jauntily wear
the sweater over his shoulders and tie the
arms loosely about his neck. But don't let this
cavalier gesture fool you. Andy is always "at
the ready," and doesn't go to the bathroom
without his cell phone strapped onto his belt.
Andy is not sexy.

 54. SKULLWEAR Keith Richards owns this look. Step off, motherf***er.

 55. "PREGNANT" MAN Guys in their third trimester should remember that it's perfectly safe to exercise up until your due date.

 56. ED HARDY–ESQUE WEAR If you are over twenty-one and now working for a living, it's the dreadful King of the Douches look. See Jon Gosselin of *Jon and Kate Plus 8* fame. Absurd. Don't be a victim. Jon, are you listening?

> " " *As the Douche said to the Trendwhore: "Bro, your Fauxhawk and Ed Hardy shirt are SICK! Let's spray ourselves with Axe and hit up Melrose." —urbandictionary.com*

> **"In the case of Jon Gosselin, everything is too big. It is what I refer to as the slobification of America. If you want to dress to feel as though you never got out of bed, then don't get out of bed."**
>
> —*TIM GUNN*, **Project Runway**

hot...or not.

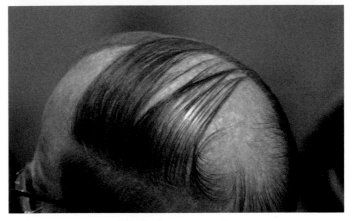

Work those strands.

 57. THE COMB-OVER Accept the fact that you are going bald with some grace. Go Google some pictures of Ed Harris to see why removing your last four pieces of hair is a kick-ass idea.

58. MULTIPLE TATTOOS This was a split decision with the women we polled. Heinous for some, a big turn-on for others. That makes this a very risky move. It really depends on what it is, where it is, what it says, et cetera. This is a big step. You really have to know what you're doing.

59. CUTOFFS Shirts or shorts. Reeks of swamps and inbreeding.

"Will wrestle gators for tips!"

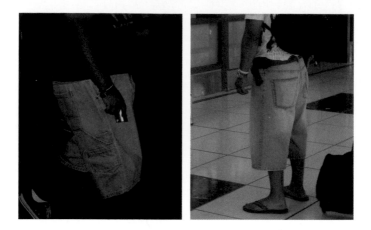

 60. JAPRI A jean capri. Baggy, calf-length jeans. Commonly worn by rappers, Kevin Federline, and misguided civilians. The ugly third cousin of jorts. Way to take a bad idea and make it longer. *(For guidance, see RED CROSS for jorts, #1.)*

61. CAUSE BRACELETS Wearing one of these in support of a friend is a really nice gesture. Stack fifteen of them up to your elbow like bangle bracelets and this look starts to lose its charm. You now have an armful of dirty smelly rubber bands. Might be time to cut 'em loose, boys.

62. THE MULLET A.K.A. "The Kentucky Waterfall." It's the old "business in the front, party in the back." Both of which you'll be doing alone.

THE TRIPLE
DECKER

GOLDY
LOCKS

THE
CAPE

 63. TUCKING ANYTHING INTO YOUR SWEATPANTS Really? Someone needs to tell you this is a bad idea? What's next, a belt?

64. TANK TOPS There's a time and a place for everything. If you want to wear a tank to the beach or the gym (and have the body to back it up), have at it. Anywhere else and you'll need to produce some sleeves if you want to be taken for anything other than a male hustler.

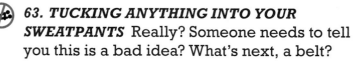 **65. DRESSING ALIKE** A picture is worth a thousand words.

 66. FAKE ROLEX A.K.A. the "Fauxlex." Let us tell you the time. It's time for you to go, MR. PHONEY BALONEY.

67. SUNGLASSES INDOORS OR AT NIGHT

> **"** Comedian Larry David put it best…"You know who wears sunglasses inside? Blind people and assholes."

68. UNFORTUNATE TIES For a guy, his tie is like a woman's breasts. It's one of the first things the opposite sex sees upon meeting you. If your tie is ugly, corny, or ragtag, you've already presented yourself as a putz. If you can't even get the tie right, we figure the worst is yet to come. (Tie help can be found at undateable.com.)

69. SPORTS SUNGLASSES/REFLECTOR BLADES/WRAPAROUNDS These "jockcessories" were designed for sports, which is where they need to stay. Worn with a suit or nice clothes, these are all wrong. And much to our dismay, a subgroup of the population known as Mega Douches have made them part of their uniform.

GQ *magazine says, "You cannot really go wrong with aviator sunglasses, no matter what the brand. They fit into that extremely rare category of 'Forever Cool.' Buy with confidence."*

*70. **THE COLUMN OF COLOR*** What are you, the Jolly Green Giant? Sure, your mother told you to "match" your clothes, but after the age of six you are expected to incorporate other colors.

*71. **NEON-COLORED CLOTHES*** Neon pink, green, and yellow belong on kids' aqua socks and Magic Markers. And that's it. No man need ever wear neon anything.

*72. **SUSPENDERS WITH A BELT*** You have missed the point of suspenders. They are used to hold up your pants...*as is a belt*. Stick with the belt. There's no contest to see how many different ways you can hold up your pants. Trust us, a man in suspenders evokes thoughts of Larry King and that is NOT the vibe we're looking for. Inside Tip: Novelty suspenders with smiley faces, musical notes, or casino cards don't make you any more fun. They make you a geek.

this isn't exactly "going green."

WHAT NOT TO BE

Benchwarmer

These guys are everywhere. Dressed in the same jersey as the players in the actual game, the Benchwarmer looks like he could jump onto the court, field, or rink at a moment's notice. He imagines the real players are his brethren, and therefore feels it's his duty to stand up and lead the crowd in the "BULLSHIT" chant after every call. He likes to scream "IN YOUR FACE" or "YEAH, BABY" while high-fiving the other sweaty, screaming Benchwarmers in his section. He's usually drunk by halftime, and likes to extol the virtues of stadium food. Like we care.

☠ **73. DUMB AND DUMBER *HAIR*** Really dumb.
P.S.: Don't forget to turn off your curling iron.

74. OVERLY GELLED HAIR Spiked-up Chia head or slicked-back Steven Seagal wannabe, any guy who is this committed to a "hairdo" is pretty much a diva. Caring too much about how your hair looks and what sort of "product" you're using is supremely unmanly. Screams "Baby wants attention."

75. PLEATED-FRONT PANTS/SHORTS No, no, and no. The only time that this is even a possibility is when the pants are the bottoms to a suit. Even then, why not just go with a plain-front suit pant? There is no way extra fabric gathered about the waist is helping your cause.

 76. HEAD-TO-TOE BLACK Black on black. You're either Guido, Johnny Cash, or have recently emerged from your suburban closet without a clue. Only works on the groovesters and rockabillies.

77. SHORT-SLEEVED DRESS SHIRT WITH A TIE We think this is what they mean by "total dweeb." Oddly enough, guys who sport this look are usually pretty smart, but you'd never know it by looking at them. There's a reason the Geek Squad at Best Buy chose this as their corporate uniform.

> **" "** *As Cary Grant once said, "If I want to wear short sleeves, I roll them up."*

 78. STUPID T-SHIRTS Tell us you can't read and we'll leave you alone.

FUCK YOU YOU FUCKIN' FUCK

FBI
FEMALE BODY INSPECTOR

DEER HUNTING

FIND ONE WITH A BIG RACK

AND MOUNT IT!

MAN OF THE MATCH

I AM THE BIG DOG DAD

© 2004 BIG DOG HOLDINGS, INC.

ADDICTED TO PORN

 79. DADDY DOESN'T LOVE ME HAIR Girlie, emo, and gothic. These fall out boys tend to be sullen and moody as well.

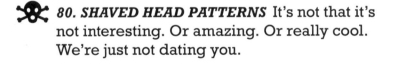 **80. SHAVED HEAD PATTERNS** It's not that it's not interesting. Or amazing. Or really cool. We're just not dating you.

81. BAD TOUPEES Is there such a thing as a good toupee? The answer is no. In this case, let yourself go bald. It's okay. Really.

 82. PERM Big mistake. Your first clue should have been when you went to the salon and realized the only other people getting perms were middle-aged housewives. If your excuse is that you didn't know this because you did a "home perm," move yourself up to KISS OF DEATH status.

☠ *83. MOHAWK* Why are we still talking about this?

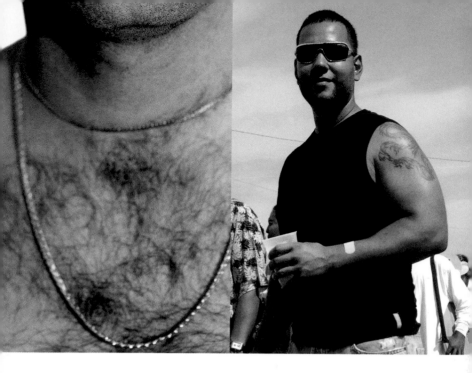

84. FAUX HAWK David Beckham can get away with this. Everyone else looks like Ed Grimley or the kid on the Big Boy Hamburger sign. Very very silly.

85. GOLD CHAINS Not big fans of gold jewelry or mancessories in general, unless it's a great watch or a plain wedding band. As for the chains—cheeseball.

86. SLEEVELESS T-SHIRTS This is another look that pretty much says it all. And by *all* we mean unsophisticated and meatheadish. Keep it at the gym.

Mr. Softy

This is the guy who spends every minute he's not in the office swathed in 100 percent cotton. This look involves ugly gray sweatpants, a T-shirt, and athletic socks. You'll notice we didn't mention any shoes, and that's because Mr. Softy rarely goes outside. He spends his entire weekend on the couch playing video games, watching sports, eating nachos, and drinking beer. When Mr. Softy asks a girl "out" for Saturday night, he's really asking her "over." Hopefully she's wearing something comfortable, too, as Mr. Softy has a "big night in" planned. This will entail watching even more television and drinking "brewskis"—you guessed it—on the couch. If she plays her cards right, there may be a pizza involved. Mr. Softy isn't one to wine and dine a girl. Why go out when he's got the most comfortable spot in the world right in front of the TV? Next to the refrigerator.

87. LEATHER PANTS Trust us, this never works unless you're Lenny Kravitz. Come on...deep in your heart, you know these are idiotic. Leather pants make you officially Undateable.

Really?

 88. FUR COAT Here's a thought...give it to us. It will make a lovely throw at the end of our bed.

89. FLOOD SHORTS Also known as "short shorts." Most boys over the age of four flat-out refuse to wear these, so why they keep showing up on adult men, we don't know. Geeky.

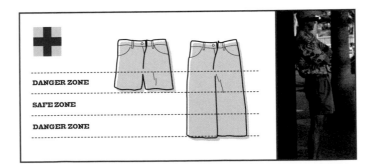

DANGER ZONE

SAFE ZONE

DANGER ZONE

 90. SUNGLASSES WORN BACKWARDS Huh?

91. BLUETOOTH If you're wearing one in your car, great. We're all for safety. It's the rest of you: walking down the street or sitting in a restaurant, waving your arms and talking loudly to an invisible friend. You look like you're either completely insane or else a pretentious ass. Neither works.

> " " *"Perhaps spending your formative years watching The Six Million Dollar Man and RoboCop gave you the mistaken impression that upgrading your body with electronics is the height of cool. Let's be clear: Walking around with a Bluetooth device in your ear is pure douchebaggery."* —Wired *magazine*

92. TUCKED-IN SWEATER This only works if the sweater is really thin and matches your skirt.

93. OVERLY TAN George Hamilton valiantly attempted this for years, and even after all that time he still couldn't pull it off. Then they voted him off *Dancing with the Stars*. Sad. There's a lesson in there somewhere. Inside Tip: Even worse are spray tans. The only reason a man should have a tan is if he's been in the sun. End of story.

94. WAXED, PLUCKED EYEBROWS This is another bizarre grooming habit of the subspecies known as "Mega Douche," page 168. Like it's not enough to wear bronzer, eyeliner, and get a pec implant…you need to pluck and wax your eyebrows, too? What's with the girlie-man routine?

95. BELLY SHIRTS We're assuming you're wearing your "midi" to show us how ripped your belly is. Congratulations on the abs. Unfortunately, you're wearing a shirt made popular by Britney Spears. See how this isn't really working out for you?

96. TACKY POLYESTER SUITS We would like to be with men who dress like they are of this era.

> " " *When Gayle K. heard we were doing this book, she said, "Please add flammable polyester suits circa 1982 to the list. Oh, and make sure to add that it was TEAL AND SHINY."*

☠ 97. THE SKULLET

That would be the bald head with long hair in
the back. There are no words.

98. _WALKING SHOES_ Orthopedic and weird. Unless you're a senior citizen on a guided tour of Pompeii, these are a major problem. Especially hideous in nude or black. Extra penalty for Velcro closures.

> _There are a lot of options here. (1) Classic bucks. Great in brown, tan, or white. (2) Classic loafers. You can't go wrong with these in cordovan. If it's above fifty degrees, skip the socks. Sexy. (3) Adidas Originals/Stan Smith white sneakers with navy trim or Rod Lavers with green trim. Old-school classics great for casual weekends, and chic enough to wear with khakis and a blazer to a dinner party. (4) Converse/Jack Purcell lo-tops. Again, old-school cool. (5) Sperry Top-Sider/Original Boat Shoe (no socks EVER with these). All of the above are never-fail, go-to casual footwear. Pair with jeans, khakis, shorts...it all works._

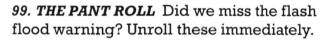 **99. _THE PANT ROLL_** Did we miss the flash flood warning? Unroll these immediately.

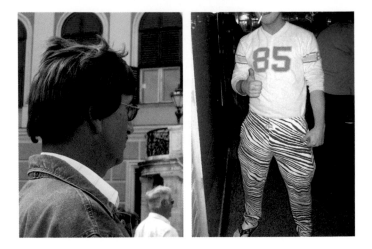

 100. DYED HAIR Here's the thing about dyed hair. If you'd like to cover a little gray and can get it done professionally, fine. If you're standing over the sink, reading directions from a box, only to end up with "brassy highlights" or wine-colored hair, you have seriously marginalized your chances of meeting a woman who will ever engage in conversation with you.

101. ZUBAZ We get it. They're "comfy." But they're also stupid, make you look stupid, and announce to the world, "I have absolutely no pride." Really, this is the clothing equivalent of a vasectomy. By the way…it's never time for "Hammer Time."

 102. PITTED-OUT SHIRTS Nothing says "cheap sweaty pig" faster than concentric yellow circles emanating from your armpit like radio waves.

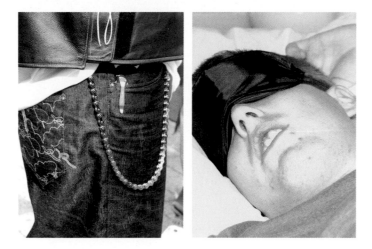

 103. CHAIN WALLET Wow, you must be a wild one. What kind of crazy sh*t are you planning for us where you need to have your wallet chained to your pants? Drag racing? A cockfight? Wrestling down a crackhead? That all sounds really fun, but we'll take a pass.

 104. SLEEPING MASK Oh yes…and will we be slathering scented moisturizer on our hands and covering them with rubber gloves before we turn in as well?

105. THE TIGHT TUCK-IN Besides a dress shirt with a suit…the only thing that needs to be tucked in this tight is a child at bedtime. Nighty-nighty to you.

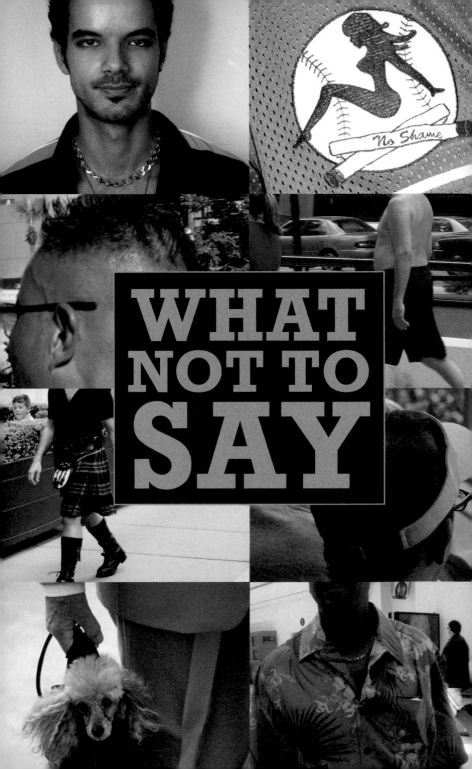

WHAT
NOT TO
SAY

One sentence or phrase can kill what might otherwise have turned into something great. And the problem here is that the possibilities are endless. A virtual bottomless pit. And you keep coming up with new ones! By far, the most damage is done in this category. You can always change your clothes...but it's harder to fix that internal filter that's supposed to censor all the bad stuff. So trust us on these.

⚑ 106. "MAKE LOVE"

✚ Just say "Have sex." No matter how many women we asked, this was the only thing that was remotely acceptable. Actually, here's a better idea—don't say anything, just do it. And by the way, don't ask if you can kiss us, either. The moment is lost.

107. "LET'S GET IT ON" Okay, Marvin Gaye. Let's not. We feel satin sheets somewhere in the midst.

108. "MY LOVER" We'd like to enact a new law: Any guy who uses this term immediately gets punched in the face.

109. "TAKE A LOAD OFF" Please just erase the word *load* from your vocabulary altogether, unless you're talking about separating colors from whites.

 110. BABY TALK ABSOLUTELY NOT. Don't even *think* about doing this. All it takes is a couple of horror-inducing sentences like "I wuv snuggling wif you. You're so comfie womfie" and you've completely annihilated what could have been something great.

 111. HOCK A LOOGIE A guttural cleaning of the throat followed by the launching of a massive ball of phlegm. The phrase alone is gag-worthy. Actually doing it—beyond unattractive.

112. FAKE SWEARING "Heck." "I'll be darned." "Jeez!" "Sheesh!" "Fudge." "Frickin'." "Daggum." Not that we want crude and crass behavior, but if the moment really truly calls for it, there's nothing that can replace the real thing. Plus, it's hard to be manly saying things like "Quit being such a gol-darned poo-poo-head pansy." See how stupid that sounded?

WHAT NOT TO BE

Meathead

Have you ever watched the show *Dog the Bounty Hunter* and thought, *Wow, that guy Dog rules?* No? Well then, chances are you're going to be equally repulsed by this freak show. Meathead barely looks human, never mind Dateable. With his roided-out, overly buffed physique (and possible bicep implants), he's basically a walking, talking action figure that should really be kept in a box somewhere. It's probably no surprise that the Meathead's disciplined lifestyle of working out, looking in the mirror, and spray-tanning hasn't left him time for much else, like reading or having conversations. In this way Meatheads are a little limited. Movies, books, world news, travel, music…all this stuff is simply a distraction for Meathead and is to be avoided at all costs. I mean, how can you count out your protein supplements if you have to pay attention to what's going on in the world? Besides, there's a lot more to life than other people and their interests and opinions. Meathead likes to focus on the important stuff, like his muscle magazine and whether his left pec is bigger today than it was yesterday. Let's face it, looking like this doesn't just happen.

*113. **BASE NAMES FOR BREASTS*** "Knockers." "Jugs." "Headlights." "Chesticles." "Abbott and Costello." "Squachies." "Milkmakers." "Magambos." "Lewinskis." "Gazongas." "Badoinkies." Just don't.

*114. **"YOU DA MAN!"*** Yelled at another person who just did something you find pleasing. For example, to LeBron James after a slam dunk, or to your cousin who finds your outboard motor on a riverbank, or to your girlfriend after excellent sex. This is usually immediately followed by an awkward or missed high five, which serves as validation that neither of you is "da man."

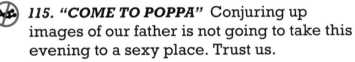

*115. **"COME TO POPPA"*** Conjuring up images of our father is not going to take this evening to a sexy place. Trust us.

*116. **"THAT REALLY CHAPS MY ASS"*** Steady there, loose cannon! Don't tell me...You don't take no guff either, do you?

*117. **"BOOB TUBE"*** And how were those three decades, living in the jungle without human contact?

*118. **"IT'S ALL GOOD"*** You may as well have a sign around your neck that says, "I have a limited vocabulary and am uncomfortable expressing myself."

119. Booya!

No one in history has ever been taken seriously after using this word. Bye-ya!

120. "TAP THAT" OR "HIT THAT"

Really? Is this what we're saying now? Seriously, you're actually picking up the phone and saying to your buddy, "I'm going to tap that ass tonight"?

*121. **"CLIT"*** No comment. Unless, of course, you can find it quickly and know what to do once it's been located. Then you can call it whatever the hell you like.

 *122. **"BEYOTCH"*** Slang for "bitch." We love when average guys try to pass this off as a normal thing to say. It's not.

 *123. **"BROS BEFORE HOES"*** As in "I can't have dinner with you and your sister tonight. I'm hittin' it with Kyle. Bros before hoes, babe." Call us if you ever reclaim your original identity. Romeo risked his family to be with Juliet. The Trojan War was waged over a woman. You're telling me that you'd rather stay home and watch reruns of *Cops* with some guy you met in traffic school than see me?

*124. **SLANG TERMS FOR VAGINA*** "Cunt." "Beaver." "Fish taco." "Twat." "Bush." "Hair clam." "Beef curtains." This would be a great opportunity to show us how fantastic you are by not using words that make our vagina sound like a rank mammal or a piece of sea life.

 TRUE STORY: "I actually know a guy whose Xbox screen name was 'Beef Curtains.' Needless to say, he spent a lot of time with his remote controls."
—*Jayne, 26, Fort Lauderdale*

125. "I MISS HIGH SCHOOL" Depressing and vaguely tragic. Plus, these are the guys who, if lucky enough to procreate, end up assaulting umpires at Little League games.

126. "THE _____STER" As a way to alter people's names. Examples: "the Zackster," "the Billster," "the Beyoncster," "the Obamster," et cetera. Can you say "disa-ster"?

127. SOPRANO-SPEAK As in "fuhgeddaboutit" and "badaboom badabing." We have to check with a therapist, but unless you're actually in the Mafia, we're pretty sure this is a legitimate mental disorder.

128. EMINEM-SPEAK It's the white guy who desperately wants to be a black rapper, so he uses terms like "sup," "li'l bro," "tru dat," "wit da," "holla," and "I's awl abou da benjamins, baby." He calls his friends his "homeys" and "dawg," and likes to imagine that he spends his time "poppin' caps" (shooting a gun) and "shakin' the bustas off" (outrunning the police), but of course, he does none of these things.

 TRUE STORY: "I was on a date with someone who is actually an upper-middle-class Jewish guy. At some point in the last year, he decided he was a black rapper. When he asked me if I wanted cream cheese on my bagel by saying, 'How about some gangsta schmear?' I knew I was in major trouble." —Sally, 31, Chicago

129. BUSINESS CLICHÉS Pointless phrases used at the office. Examples: "You're really pushing the envelope there, Kelly!" "Let's get on the same page." "Let me run it up the flagpole." "Come on, people, think outside the box!" You might think using these in a meeting demonstrates that you're on top of things. What it actually says is, "I don't have an original thought in my head."
INSIDE TIP: If you actually make a habit of talking like this in the workplace, there's a 99 percent chance that at some point, when you were out of your office, at least one co-worker has rubbed his genitalia on your keyboard in retribution.

130. "THE FAMILY JEWELS" We get it. They're precious. Perhaps a good knee to the groin will put an end to this gem.

WHAT NOT TO BE

Bitter Boy

Bitter Boy isn't so much a look as it is a mind-set. First off, let's just get this out of the way: Bitter Boy has personally never done anything wrong. Ever. It's the rest of us who are f***ing everything up and making his life a living hell. His boss is a "total douche" and doesn't know his "ass from a hole in the ground." The guy who delivers his mail is a "f***ing idiot who can't do anything right," the senior citizen who lives above him is a "complete dick," and all his previous girlfriends are "crazy bitches." Perhaps Bitter Boy's biggest enemy is a vague and ever-present force known as "they." "They" are always ruining everything, keeping Bitter Boy down and driving this country right into the ground. "They" are making it so that a guy like Bitter Boy can barely function, let alone make a living. Never mind that Bitter Boy, by virtue of being a white, able-bodied male, has won the genetic lottery. Forget that BB's ancestors have never been oppressed and have been running the country since it started. That's irrelevant. What isn't fair is how Bitter Boy has to live where those f***ing cabdrivers can't even speak the language and the world's dumbest dry cleaner takes forever to get his shirts back. F***!

131. "MOIST" There is no reason for a man to ever use this word. Or a woman, for that matter. It may, however, be read silently to yourself from the back of a small toilette package.

132. "NOT THAT I KNOW OF" In response to the question "Do you have any children?" Yup, this kind of devil-may-care attitude toward one's offspring is what we all look for in the perfect male companion.

133. "BONER" This word hurts our ears, as do "I've got a chubby," "hard-on," "pitch a tent," "stiffy," and even "erection." We know what's going on down there; you don't have to tell us. Also, please spare us the "I popped a..." in front of any of these terms.

134. SPORTS METAPHORS As applied to everyday situations that have nothing to do with sports. Examples: "Knock it out of the park." "Let's not lose sight of the goal line." "Time to water the infield." (This is a "fun" way to order another round.) "It's a home run." "Tonight's going to be a slam dunk."

> " " Jack Nicholson put it perfectly in the movie As Good as It Gets when he said, "People who speak in metaphors ought to shampoo my crotch."

⚡ 135. "IN YOUR FACE!"

Especially when accompanied by an
exuberant finger point and a flushed red
face. If you do this while playing sports with
your buddies, chances are they secretly hate
you. If a girl sees you, she thinks, *Freak show*

136. GROSS TERMS FOR MENSTRUAL CYCLE

"On the rag." "Riding the white saddle." "The crimson tide." "Riding the crimson wave." "Cherry juice." "Cousin red." "Ride the cotton pony." "Fallen to the Communists." Usually said while drinking beer in the presence of other men, as in "Couldn't get any last night, Christie's on the rag." If you value your life, pray that no woman ever hears you say this. It won't be pretty.

137. SOPHOMORIC EXPRESSIONS FOR GOING TO THE BATHROOM

"Take a dump." "Put some duds in a box." "Drop the kids off at the pool." "Burn a mule." "Layin' some pipe." "Take the Browns to the Super Bowl." "Squeeze out a steamer." "Take a dooker." "Drop a deuce." "Gotta take a piss." "Drain the main vein." "Drain the dragon." "Shake hands with a legend." "Take a whiz." "Gotta squirt." "Go see a man about a horse." The worst.

 At this point, we'd like to mention that there's no need to describe or inform anyone of what you are actually going to do in the bathroom. You don't even have to tell us where you're going. A simple "Excuse me for a moment" is all that's necessary.

138. JUVENILE NAMES FOR SPERM "Cum." "Jizz." "Spooge." "Baby batter." "Man juice." "Penis pudding." "Cream." All just foul.

139. "BUST A NUT" To work really hard, as in "I busted a nut" on that project. You know what else is a bust? This date.

 140. PET NAMES FOR YOUR PENIS "Big Jim." "Love muscle." "One-eyed monster." "Trouser snake." "Schlong." "My Johnson." "The Captain." "Little Stevie." "Herman the One-Eyed German." "Willy." "Rod." Icky and gross. You and "Junior" need to have a little heart-to-heart and get a new game plan. Like silence.

141. NASTY GUY TALK "Cock block." "Titty f***." "Blue balls." "Jack off." "Just the tip." "Double-bagger." "Butterface." "Spank bank." "Shot my wad." "Spank the monkey." Et cetera. Talk like this and you are no longer Dateable. They are repulsive, rank phrases that make our skin crawl. If you must speak like this, keep it in the locker room. While we're at it—why is there a need to say things like "rub one out," "beat your meat," "play the skin flute," and "buff the helmet"? Not that the word *masturbate* is so delightful...but trust us, you're just making it worse.

 142. SKANKY TERMS FOR SEX "Lay some pipe." "Get your rocks off." "Hot beef injection." "Porked." "Popped her cherry." And the ever-lovely "I balled her." Charming.

come here often?

143. LAME PICKUP LINES "Have you been working out? Because you've been running through my mind all day." "Were you arrested earlier? It's gotta be illegal to look that good." "I'm no Fred Flintstone, but I could make your bed rock." "That shirt's very becoming on you. But if I was on you I'd be coming, too." "I don't have a library card, but do you mind if I check you out?" "Was your father an alien? Because there's nothing else like you on earth." THESE NEVER WORK.

 144. FOREIGN PHRASES (REAL AND IMAGINED) Examples: "Ciao!" when saying good-bye to a friend on the street in Chicago. "Squattez-vous" as a way to say "sit down" in faux French. "*Merci* buckets," a *hilarious* riff on *merci beaucoup,* the French phrase for "thank you very much." A foreign language isn't a free pass for you to act like a complete ass. It's simply a different language. No need to spaz out here.

145. "HOW'S IT HANGING?" You've just greeted another man by asking him if his penis is doing okay between his two balls. Does this seem odd to anyone besides us?

 146. GIVE SOMEONE A "KNUCKLE SANDWICH" Anyone using the term *knuckle sandwich* isn't punching anyone. He'll more likely run home crying after he gets his ass kicked.

 147. "MY OLD LADY" Acceptable to say to your girl only after she's done a nice job tidying up the family meth lab.

 148. "THE BIG KAHUNA" In reference to a man's status in the world. Example: "My boss is the BIG KAHUNA." When you say it, we think, *BIG TOOL.*

149. "PUBES" Next, please.

150. SERIOUSLY REFERRING TO YOUR "INNER CHILD" There is no "inner child," only an idiotic inner adult who won't stop speaking in psychobabble and clichés.

151. *TALKING ABOUT YOURSELF IN THE THIRD PERSON* This odd habit was made popular by Bob Dole when he was running for president in 1996. He would say things like "You're going to see the real Bob Dole from now on in," or "Bob Dole isn't some sort of fringe candidate." To speak of yourself as a separate person from yourself is moving into a territory commonly known as "crazy business."

152. *"MAIN SQUEEZE"* What are we, a roll of Charmin now?

153. *SPEAKING ENGLISH LOUDLY TO FOREIGNERS IN THE HOPE THEY WILL UNDERSTAND YOU BETTER* The only thing that translates is that you are a complete 'nad.

154. *SPEAKING IN THE VOICE OF A CARTOON CHARACTER* Whether it's Bugs Bunny ("That's all, folks") or Popeye ("I am what I am"), it doesn't matter. We are so embarrassed for you we literally don't know where to look.

> **TRUE STORY:** *"Last summer my roommate started dating a pretty cute guy, but the more they went out the more he talked in the voice of Snagglepuss. It got so his only reply to anything was 'Sufferin' succotash.' He would only do this during the day, never at night. At night he was completely normal, so we ended up calling him Daytime Snagglepuss, which then got shortened to Daytime. Needless to say, we're done here."*

Easy, Jedi...

155. "MAY THE FORCE BE WITH YOU"
Quoting the made-up philosophies of the made-up Obi-Wan Kenobi in earnest is a surefire way to launch your weirdo quotient into the stratosphere.

> **TRUE STORY:** "I was at my boyfriend's Monday-night softball game, and a player from the other team got up to bat. The score was tied, and things were getting a little tense, when out of nowhere the batter's teammate, in all seriousness, screams, 'USE THE FORCE!!!' " –Megan, 26, Chicago

> " " Kyle McCarthy, writer for the Royal Order of Experience Design, puts it this way: "Look, we've all at some time or another wished the Force was real, and we were its Master. But some shit you just keep to yourself, okay?"

156. INSIDER NAMES FOR DRUGS "Horse." "Sweet Lucy." "420." "Smack." "Eight-Ball." "Alice B. Toklas." "B-bomb." "Cat in the Hat." We see you as a skanky druggie or a geek who likes to think he's "down with the street lingo."

157. "MAJOR _____AGE" As a way to indicate a large quantity of something. Examples: "Whoa, major boobage on that chick." "My cell phone is getting major barage right here." "I'm ready for a vacation. I've had major jobage lately." Know what else you have? Major aloneage.

158. SILLY NAMES FOR DIARRHEA "The trots." "The Hershey squirts." "The chocolate faucet." "Blow mud." "The Air and Water Show." Do you boys have to tell us everything?

159. NAMING FARTS "SBD" (silent but deadly). "Trouser trumpet." "Rip ass." "The rectal honk." "One-gun salute." "Blast the chair." "Blow the big brown horn." "Bottom burp." "Float an air biscuit." "Crack one off." "Sneak one out." "Crop dusting." Here's a thought: Why don't you go air yourself out and not come back?

160. UNAMUSING NAMES FOR THE BATHROOM "The Shitter." "The John." "The Little Boys' Room." "The Can." "The Head." "The Shit House." "The Throne." Don't feel obligated to come back.

161. QUOTING LINES FROM MOVIES IN CHARACTER This is beyond painful. The most commonly imitated characters are the Godfather ("I'll make you an offer you can't refuse") and the Terminator ("*Hasta la vista,* baby" and "I'll be back"). Lastly, and guaranteed to be the most excruciating three minutes ever spent on the planet, a guy doing the Joe Pesci "clown scene" from *GoodFellas:* "What, am I a clown? Do I amuse you?" And don't even get us started on Borat...

162. CORNY NAMES FOR CITIES "The Big Apple." "La-La Land." "San Fran." "Chi-town." "The Motor City." "Beantown." "Tinseltown." "Sin City." "The Big Easy." Stop it. You sound like a high school cheerleader on her first airplane ride.

163. "BEJESUS" As in, "Wow, that sudden clap of thunder scared the bejesus out of me!" Now we're actually concerned about your ability to keep it together. Are you going to have a breakdown if it starts raining?

164. MADE-UP WORDS "Chillaxin'." "Anyhoo." "Ginormous." "Redonkulous." "Dealio." This is a really quick way to end a date.

> *TRUE STORY: Our friend Joe G, a respected financial adviser, works with a guy who says things like "This is a ginormous piece of business." Joe says, "This is a man who sits down to pee and wears an apron."*

165. "YEAH, BABY" (A) As bellowed at the game on the television or to the waitress when she delivers food or drinks. We'll bet you a thousand dollars that the guy who yells this is drunk, wearing a backward baseball cap, and guilty of at least twenty of the Undateables found in this book.

166. "YEAH, BABY" (B) Austin Powers style. Not many people can do a great Austin Powers imitation, so your date might not understand that you are imitating a complete dork and skip right to thinking *you* are the complete dork. Careful here.

167. DATED TERMS FOR THE INTERNET "Surf the Web." "The Information Superhighway." "The Interweb." "The Internets." "Cyberspace." Where the hell have you been for the last fifteen years?

168. "A BUTTLOAD" OF ANYTHING How much stuff can you put in your butt? You're talking about it like it's a supertanker.

169. "KNOW MY ASS FROM A HOLE IN THE GROUND" You'd have to be really f***ing stupid to get these two mixed up.

170. "TCB" You might be "taking care of business" but we're taking a cab. BUH-BYE.

171. "BREWSKI"

This word must be stricken from your vocabulary the minute you hit twenty-one.

172. "I'M A HAPPY CAMPER" You're also the guy whose personal mission is to bring a little sunshine into everyone's day. We have four words for you: SHUT. YOUR. PIE. HOLE.

173. "JUST JOSHIN' YA" What, is "just joking" too risqué for you? Highly nerdly.

174. "I FEEL YOU" WITH DOUBLE FIST TO THE HEART BUMP Unless you just won the Super Bowl and you're celebrating in the locker room, don't do this.

175. "BEAMER" Yuppie poser left over from the 1980s.

176. "LET'S BOOGIE"

Let me introduce myself: I'm a horny guy trying to get laid. Or wo— a horny guy who wants to dance. Slow your roll, Barry Gibb.

177. "I'M STARVIN' LIKE MARVIN"

177. "STRAP ON THE FEED BAG"; "I'M STARVIN' LIKE MARVIN" A simple "I'm really hungry" will suffice here.

 178. "OKELY DOKELY" Emulating Ned Flanders is not hot. Whoopsie daisies!

179. "COOL BEANS" Even the eleven-year-old girls who popularized this phrase now think it's so five minutes ago.

180. "CRUISIN' FOR A BRUISIN'" This is in no way intimidating or threatening. Actually, at this point, we're pretty sure we could take you.

181. "COP A SQUAT" What are we, on a stakeout? Working in a rice paddy? Lighting a campfire? We assure you, no one is interested in doing any "squatting" at the moment. Whatever happened to "Would you like to sit down?"

182. "PEACE OUT"

> *Working every presumably hip phrase in existence into your repertoire doesn't make you cool. It makes you a follower. Girls like a leader. Be original.*

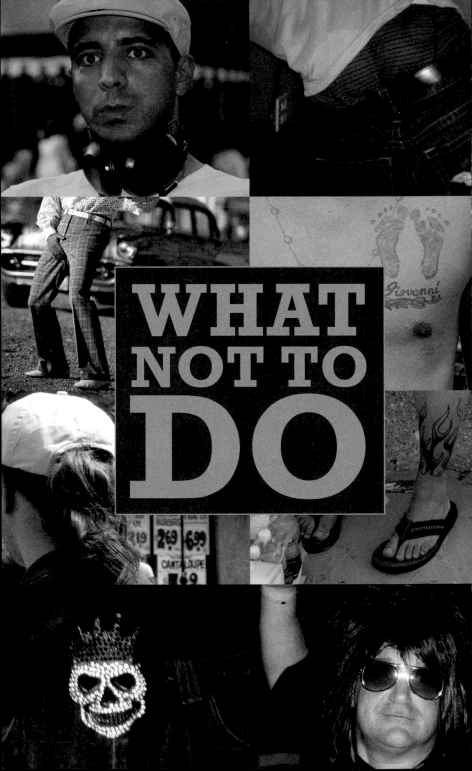

WHAT
NOT TO
DO

By now you're totally sick
of us, so we'll skip the intro.
Just stop doing all this stuff,
okay?

Have you met my cat Carol?   *Hey big guy!*

 183. OWN A CAT If it belonged to your grandmother who asked you to take care of it before she died, or you found it on the street, felt sorry for it, and took it in, then fine. Even somewhat adorable. If you deliberately went to a pet store and bought a cat, that's a problem.

 184. THE "GOTCHA" That would be the wink, the tongue click, and the trigger motion, followed by the word "Gotcha." The gesture is often used to imply "I got you covered," "I hear you," "I agree with you," et cetera. What it really says is "I'm a huge dork."

 185. OWN A VIOLENT DOG Scary. We're guessing you have multiple neck tattoos and wear a choke collar as well. And how do you know that thing isn't going to go completely psycho and rip our spleen out?

 186. PT CRUISERS The fact that a single guy was ever talked into buying one of these cars is a miracle.

 187. ANYTHING SCENIC PAINTED ONTO YOUR VEHICLE Whatever inspired you to have a wolf perched on a cliff, howling at the moon, painted on your car is truly a mystery. Same goes for flames. Let's call this what it is…a guy with a lot of extra time and a little extra cash.

> *"At a Chicago Bears game, we saw a mural of a full-size grizzly bear ripping Brett Favre in half painted on the side of an RV. Absolutely transcendent on game day, a bit sad every other day."*
> —Jamie F., videographer

188. SHAVE YOUR CHEST Let us guess. You work out three hours a day, self-tan, wear wraparound sunglasses, and think you're hot. P.S.: "Chest stubble" is nasty.

 189. PLAY DUNGEONS & DRAGONS Telling a girl you're a "Dungeon Master" might freak her out. Just a thought. INSIDE TIP: This also applies to online versions of the game, like World of Warcraft. Now you're just a digital dork.

 190. PAINT YOUR FACE FOR A SPORTING EVENT Even worse, painting your chest or body. You're breaking two rules here—going shirtless in public and painting yourself.

191. "PULL A PLUMBER" Your pants have slid four inches below the top of your pale, hairy butt crack. Even if we've seen all of your butt before, we'll still react as if we've seen a dead animal on the side of the road.

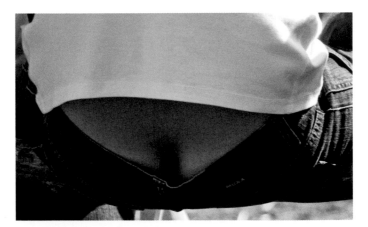

✪ 192. ATTEND STAR TREK CONVENTIONS

Trekkies need to give it up by age eighteen. And while we're at it, let's put an end to the wizard and *Star Wars* conventions. It's all weird and geeky. Try taking us with you or talking about it on a date, and here's what we'll say: "Live long and prosper. Alone."

193. *OVERLY CREATIVE VOICE-MAIL MESSAGE* We can only imagine how much time this must have taken...writing out the copy, finding the perfect music and the right sound effects, and performing it at least ten times until it's just right. Know what else we can imagine? Leaving you a really creative "No thank you" message.

194. *GET DRUNK ON PLANE* This is always fun, because there's no way we can get away from you. Not only are you a boozy blowhard talking incessantly about nothing, but we also have to smell your breath for hours on end. Vile.

195. *LEAVE PORN LYING AROUND THE HOUSE* Slimeball. Extra penalty for *Juggs*, touted as "The dirtiest tit-mag in the world." And by the way, who the hell looks at porn in a magazine anymore anyway? Buy a computer and watch it online.

196. *GO ON AN "IRON JOHN" WEEKEND* Taking your fair share of "mancations," such as golfing, fishing, or skiing trips with your friends, is fantastic. Beating a drum, chanting relentlessly, and sweating naked in a hot box to get in touch with your inner man, as an attempt to connect with the "men's movement," is not. Let's rein it in here.

197. DIRTY CAR Gross. If your car's a mess, chances are you're a mess, too. Spend the fifteen bucks and get it cleaned if you are serious about dating.

198. MOOBS A.K.A. "man boobs," "chest gout," "the maternity gourd." We don't know what to tell you. You look awful naked as well as in clothes. There's nowhere (and no way) to hide. Perhaps a toga? Binding your chest with duct tape? You really need to get on this.

> **" "** *The fully developed man bosom can cause a great deal of Oedipal confusion. Do we nuzzle our head in there or call child services?"*
> —Details *magazine*

Nice Rack.

199. UNDERTIP...AND THEN EXPLAIN WHY IT'S OKAY Here's a tip: Unless the waitperson threw a cup of scalding coffee in your face, leaving you so disfigured that you are now unemployable, leave at least 10 percent. Otherwise, 15 to 20 percent is what hardworking people deserve. And by the way, *don't* pull the whole "What do you think, 5 percent tip? The coffee was cold" trick to make it seem like a group decision. We will *not* be an accomplice to your stinginess.

200. FAIL TO PAY ON THE FIRST DATE Once you've been on a few dates, it's okay to let the woman suggest splitting the bill. (We're not saying you should take her up on it, but it isn't completely inappropriate to entertain the thought.) But not paying on the first date means there won't be a second one.

> " " *As the sassy girls behind the counter at Chicago's famed Wiener's Circle say, "Bitches don't pay."*

201. OVERLY BUFFED This says, "I have absolutely no interests, hobbies, or friends outside the gym. I would sleep next to the free weights if they would let me." The other problem is that your bulging physique is freaky looking. You think you come off as a stud, but really, you're more like a brainless cartoon character.

202. GO SHIRTLESS IN PUBLIC

It doesn't work on the jogging path, at the baseball game, or walking down the street. We don't care what the temperature is. The only acceptable places to be shirtless are at the beach, in the shower, and in bed.

203. ORDER A GIRLIE DRINK

Kahlúa and Cream, Grasshoppers, Mango Martinis…all wrong. Stick to beer, wine, vodka and tonics, scotch and soda, and so on. Margaritas are fine.

> *Before ordering, ask yourself the following: If Frank Sinatra or Steve McQueen were here, would he kick your ass if you ordered this drink?*

204. _FULL-BODY WAX_ Unless you're attempting to break some sort of world speed record and are required to be as aerodynamic as possible, this is just bizarre for all the same reasons as shaving your chest. Wax unwanted hair in trouble spots, but keep it to yourself. A full-body wax is nothing short of a FREAK SHOW.

 205. _OWN A RODENT_ Gerbils, rats, ferrets, mice...another really hard concept to grasp. And stop forcing us to hold them and "admit" that they're cute. They're not cute. They're disgusting. So off the mark here.

206. _PLAY AIR GUITAR_ It is impossible to look cool doing this. If you really want to impress us, learn to play the real guitar. Even better, play a real guitar and _get paid_ for it.

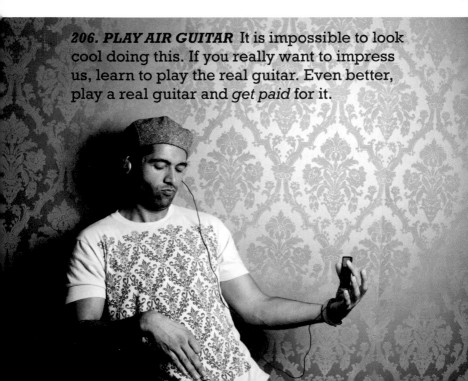

207. ENTER DUMB CONTESTS No one wants to see you try to eat the most hot dogs or win a tote bag.

208. BRING A BASEBALL GLOVE TO A PROFESSIONAL GAME What are you going to do—elbow the little kids out of the way to grab a foul ball? If you're over fifteen, this is highly suspect.

> *You catch a foul ball with that glove and you'll probably get some applause from the fans in your section. Maybe you'll be on the replay screen. But you're definitely losing the respect of every other guy there who knows the only acceptable way to catch a foul ball is bare-handed.*

209. REARRANGE YOUR JUNK IN PUBLIC

A.K.A. "pocket pool." At some point, we've probably had to endure an explanation of how your private parts have a tendency to lean left or right. Don't care. Go to the men's room and get it together.

210. PERSONALIZED CELL PHONE RING

If you must, then you need to choose wisely. Depending on the song, this can either move you forward or send the evening crashing to the ground like a flaming zeppelin. "SexyBack"—not good. "Funky Cold Medina"—funny. We don't know why. That's just how it is.

211. "THE CLUB" STEERING WHEEL LOCK (1)

Do you not have insurance? (2) If your car is really that special, engage the valet and tip him well. (3) If the neighborhood is that bad, why are we here?

212. LACTOSE-INTOLERANT

This is another way to say "Wimpy farter." And please, don't regale us with the fascinating details of what you had for lunch and how it's affecting your intestines.

213. READ MUSCLE MAGAZINES

And who can blame you! Forget the newspaper, *Esquire*, *GQ*, *Time*, and *Newsweek*. This issue has even more roided-out freaks than last month!

WHAT NOT TO BE

Enlightened Guy

Fortified by way too many self-help books and spiritual group sessions, most likely wearing a bracelet "with special meaning," Enlightened Guy walks the earth spreading his pointless and off-topic psychobabble everywhere he goes. This is the guy who speaks in metaphors, quotes emotional gibberish, and asks "deep" and random questions, none of which make any sense. "Where have all the children gone?" he'll query while staring at a garbage truck. He also says moronic things like "I'm in a really good/bad/scary place right now," "I need to respect my inner child," and "No one walks alone if love is pure." What?!? With his soulful expression and precious thoughts, not only is Enlightened Guy impossible to talk to, but he's got about as much sex appeal as a Hello Kitty pencil case. Quoting Deepak Chopra, doing yoga, crying...it's like dating a teenage girl. If you ask Enlightened Guy what it is he's trying to say, he'll just sigh ruefully and stare off into the horizon. Do you know why he does this? Because he doesn't have a clue what he's talking about, either. Enlightened Guy has inhaled so much self-indulgent, overly dramatic nonsense, he can't answer a simple question like "Where are the hamburger buns?" without quoting Gandhi. This guy needs to be air-dropped into a dark canyon full of wild, hungry coyotes and be made to claw his way out. Perhaps this will give him a new reality-based understanding of the word "needs." Incredibly unmanly and beyond annoying. If you date one of these guys, you just might have to end the night by beating his ass.

214. PREMATURELY BUSTING OUT PORN

Keep this to yourself until there is some indication that the girl is even remotely interested. Just because she doesn't dress like a Pilgrim doesn't mean she's into porn. She's going to have to say something as direct as "Do you have any sexy movies we can watch?" for you to move ahead. If there is a porn "collection" lurking somewhere, keep it under lock and key, and introduce it in small doses. Anything else and we'll think *Perv.*

215. CHEESY ONLINE DATING "HANDLES"

Quite a few women have decent luck meeting guys online. They are, however, completely grossed out by some of the handles used. Three minutes on Match.com introduced us to "Sexy," "Hot Love," "Black Diamond Guy," and "Mr. Scratch." Remember, you're trying to *get* a date.

216. COMPLAIN ABOUT MONEY TROUBLES

Not on the first date. Not on the tenth date. Never would be great.

 217. VANITY PLATES You know who rocks vanity plates? Soccer moms. Girlie and self-important.

 218. NOVELTY STEERING WHEEL COVERS This includes fuzzy fake fur, leather, and pleather. What, a regular steering wheel doesn't work for you? Why is this even remotely necessary? And if your hands get that sweaty from simply driving a car, that's a whole other issue we're not particularly interested in dealing with.

219. RADIO TUNED TO LITE FM OR EASY-LISTENING STATION Ugh, getting into a guy's car and hearing the sultry tones of Kenny G is really more than one can bear. What's next, Yanni? Actually, let's just save each other a lot of time and effort and call it a night.

220. "GO DUTCH" We don't know what's worse, the concept or the phrase.

 221. CAR TCHOTCHKES Dice, air fresheners, bobble-head dolls, Beanie Babies, hood ornaments…You know how little girls put streamers on the handlebars of their pink Sting-Rays? This is the same thing.

 222. STUPID BUMPER STICKERS Thanks for sharing your "wacky" sense of humor with us. The downside is that now everyone knows you're a complete idiot before you even get out of the car.

 223. SISSY DRIVING If a guy is tentative and awkward behind the wheel, he'll be tentative and awkward in bed.

> **" "** *As a world-famous comedian once said, "You can find out everything you need to know about a man by the way he drives."*

 224. REFERRING TO YOUR CAR AS "SHE" As in "Look at her. Isn't she a beauty?" Yes, "she" is, but your car is not alive. Nor is it a woman.

✸ 225. ROAD RAGE

"You f***ing prick! I'm going to f***ing kill you. I'm going to f***ing shove a golf club so far up your ass that it comes out of your mouth. F*** you! You f***ing dumb motherf***er! Suck my dick, f***head!!!" Somehow this wasn't the conversation we were envisioning on the way to dinner.

226. THE V GESTURE Yes, we're talking about the tongue, the peace sign, and the tongue wiggle. There are much better ways to admire someone or say hello.

 227. THE JACK-OFF GESTURE Especially charming when accompanied by "Suck my dick" or "Blow me." But there's a silver lining here: You're at least practicing for all those nights you won't be having sex.

228. THE BLOW-JOB GESTURE Simultaneously pushing your tongue into the side of your cheek and sliding your fist over an imaginary horizontal pole is possibly the most low-end behavior imaginable. Doing this pretty much ensures you won't be getting one.

229. ATTEND MEDIEVAL TIMES OR A MEDIEVAL FESTIVAL An afternoon of falconry, heavy-duty leather, and the strumming of a mandolin is too twisted to even contemplate. M'lady says not a chance.

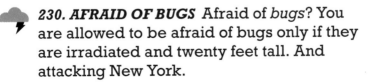 ***230. AFRAID OF BUGS*** Afraid of *bugs*? You are allowed to be afraid of bugs only if they are irradiated and twenty feet tall. And attacking New York.

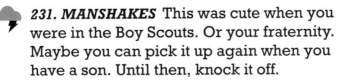 ***231. MANSHAKES*** This was cute when you were in the Boy Scouts. Or your fraternity. Maybe you can pick it up again when you have a son. Until then, knock it off.

 232. "JACKED-UP" CAR How does this happen? You buy a car and then you decide it needs to be three feet higher? We don't get it. And furthermore, we prefer not to use a ladder to get into a car.

 233. CREEPILY INTO MOM Here's the deal...if you take Mom out for special brunch dates, accompany her on a relaxing cruise through the Greek Isles (her treat), and say things about her like "She's a keeper," you are accidentally dating your mom. The good news is you don't need to find a girlfriend because you already have one.

 234. PUBLICLY TAKE BEANO First of all, isn't there some other product that can help you? Something that actually sounds like medicine? When you find out what that is, take it and keep it to yourself. No one cares.

✖ 235. OWN A TOY DOG

Get rid of it or get a man dog. If you're transporting it in a designer carry-on, you have jumped to KISS OF DEATH status. *Note: If you dress your "doggie," now that she's all dolled up, why don't you just take her out to dinner?*

236. *BALD-AWAY*

Basically, this is spray-painting your bald spot. Again, the inherent problem is that this behavior is much like wearing a toupee or hanging on to your mangy little strands of hair and combing them over... JUST GO BALD. Any woman worth her salt understands that confidence, not hair, is what makes the man.

237. *HAIR CLUB FOR MEN* Quit. Hard to believe, but this special "hair club" still exists. When our friend Lindsey commented on her date's hair and he launched into the details of his HCFM membership, she told us she knew it was time for a "family emergency." See Kiss of Death.

238. *DISTURBING LAUGH* Loud guffawing, high-pitched giggling, snorting, seal barks, et cetera. A hard one to get past. You're going to have to be really funny or really great in bed to have this move forward.

239. *BITE OR CHEW NAILS* Repulsive. And if it involves toenails, we can't even speak.

240. BAD DANCING Jerking around like a tasered giraffe and having no rhythm usually signals issues in other areas. We know it can be hard to be a good dancer, so find a basic move and just stick with it. Otherwise, it's safer to buy the drinks and watch from the sidelines.

 241. "SERIOUSLY GOOD" DANCER You are way into dancing. One minute we're at a wedding having a drink, and then next thing we know you're on the dance floor doing the Moonwalk or busting out a Soulja Boy that would guarantee you a spot as one of Justin Timberlake's backup dancers. Actually, you are so into it, you don't even notice us leaving the building and driving away in sheer humiliation. Note: The Cabbage Patch is OVER.

242. PICK BUTT IN PUBLIC Use your head here. Just because you scan the room and don't see anyone looking doesn't give you permission to launch a search-and-rescue mission between your buns. If things are that twisted up, go to the men's room and get it handled.

243. ONLY GO TO BYOB RESTAURANTS Cheap bastard. And just so you know, your little monologue on how no restaurant in the entire city serves your special vintage isn't fooling anybody.

244. *MORTIFYING FACIAL EXPRESSIONS WHILE DANCING* The White Man's Overbite. Pursed lips. Grimacing. "Orgasm" face. Just know we're dying to get off the dance floor while doing our best to act like you're not our date.

245. PLASTIC BAGS OR BOXES AS "LUGGAGE" A.K.A. "the Alabama Suitcase." If you get off a plane carrying this, you will be returning home sooner than you could have ever imagined.

 246. OWN A VAN Minivans or utility trucks —we're not real psyched to be picked up in either. Note: Windowless vans are creepy. Evokes memories of the scene in *The Silence of the Lambs* when Buffalo Bill kidnaps the senator's daughter by tricking her into his van. You know what's really not all that romantic a movie? *The Silence of the Lambs*.

247. ASSUME YOU'RE "GETTING SOME" ON THE FIRST DATE Way too cocky and completely mistaken.

 248. EYE LIFT/FACE-LIFT On a man? No! We don't care how good your doctor is, you will end up looking like a pampered woman. Again, we like our men a little askew.

249. POPPED COLLAR
It was bad enough back
in the day when actual
polo-wearing preppies
used this gesture as
a way to broadcast
their supposed WASPy
superiority. The fact
that some of you are
now imitating those
pastel-wearing posers to suggest you too
are part of the same uber-elitist contingency
makes you twice as bad. They were genuine
tools. You're a fake tool.

 **250. WHIP OUT A CALCULATOR AT DINNER
TO SPLIT THE CHECK** Beyond mortifying. The
only thing that could make this more cringe-
worthy is to bust out a laminated tip card.
INSIDE TIP: Forget women not liking guys who
do this...*nobody* likes guys who do this.

 251. BLOW NOSE LOUDLY Please take this
disgusting gesture outside or to the men's
room.

 252. PREP FOR SEX Satin sheets, sexy music,
dim lights, mirrors on the ceiling...creepy.
We're all for romantic, but your "one-night sex
package" routine isn't making us feel all that
special. Something tells us you've done this
before. Often.

 253. CREEPY BODYBUILDING SUPPLEMENTS
Weird powders that get made into shakes,
mysterious "enhancers," and hundreds of
vitamins, all probably chock-full of steroids
and coated with Hulk Hogan's armpit sweat.
And then a ninety-minute dissertation on how
this will help you grow more muscle. GOTTA
GO! The only person you should be dating is
your spotter.

 254. CARRY A PLAYING BOOM BOX Why do
you think that everyone within fifty feet wants
to listen to your music? This is really just a
call for help from someone who can't function
unless he's the center of attention. We all like
music. But keep it turned down, preferably
inside your house. Better yet, get some
headphones.

**255. SPEND HALF THE DAY FORWARDING
INTERNET JOKES** Or worse, Internet porn.
You most certainly have better things to do at
work. Stop sending the nude e-mails. Unless
it's Megan Fox.

256. WON'T VALET/DRIVES AROUND LOOKING FOR PARKING SPOT
Sure, no problem, we'd love to walk six blocks and destroy a two-hundred-dollar pair of heels so you can save eight bucks. But if you have to do this, at least drop us off first, then go look for a spot. That way, while we're waiting for you at the bar, we can maybe meet a nice guy who's not a total tightwad.

257. HALF-OFF COUPON ON DATE
Also known as a "twofer." Never. Ever. If you are a "coupon clipper," this is a dirty little secret you must take to the grave. We all know that little coupon isn't just a coupon. It's a glimpse into our future with you. A future filled with early-bird specials, and Pick 'N Pair Lunch Combos at Applebee's. Not exactly the stuff dreams are made of.

258. OVERLY COMPLICATED FOOD ORDERS
"I'll have the chicken Parmesan, no skin, no oil on the chicken, fresh tomatoes, a little basil, light mozzarella, a side of pasta, again no oil, not too cooked, hold the garlic, a little lemon, yogurt instead of cream"…BLAH! BLAH! BLAH! Did you happen to notice our eyes rolling into the back of our heads and the blood dripping out of our ears? Feel free to revive us with smelling salts after this incredibly dull and self-indulgent monologue is over.

259. COMPLAIN ABOUT COST OF DATE WHILE ON A DATE
You're right, this is expensive. I'll have the lobster.

WHAT NOT TO BE

Stoney

Stoneys always start out great. With their thick shaggy hair, nice eyes, and easygoing nature, these guys usually have a certain appeal. "That's cool," "Just chillin'," and "No problem" are the Stoney's mantras. A lot of Stoneys are actually pretty athletic, and tend to be into the outdoors...hiking, biking, surfing, or "just soaking up the rays." Dressing mostly for their sport of choice, Stoneys usually end up with a pretty decent wardrobe. Fleece jackets, board shorts, faded jeans, flip-flops, cool sunglasses...it's all good. The problems start when you realize Stoney doesn't think more than forty-five minutes into the future. Things like being on time, having a job, money...not important to Stoney. To his credit, Stoney doesn't need much cash. Since he always has a roommate, his rent tends to be minimal. Stoney doesn't own a car because he bikes, skateboards, or "bums a ride" wherever he needs to go, and he's usually fed by sympathetic friends. The way Stoney sees it, he just needs to make enough money to pursue his one true passion...pot. You will find that most of his phone calls, conversations, errands, and hobbies revolve around pot. Stoney's idea of a perfect day? Smoking pot. Stoney's idea of a fun date? Stopping off at a friend's barbecue (free food), hitting a street fair (free entertainment), and smoking pot. Stoneys are perfect for the here and now. And by that we mean the next two hours. If you're wondering what life is going to look like in two years, don't ask Stoney. He definitely can't see it.

260. VIGOROUSLY RUBBING PALMS TOGETHER IN ANTICIPATION OF ANYTHING

You can do this only if you're a supervillain who just perfected a dastardly device that controls the weather. Seeing a plate of ribs or the opening credits to a movie shouldn't produce this response in a reasonably well-adjusted male.

261. OWN A BONG (IF OVER THIRTY)

Doesn't sit well with the women, and gives you away as someone who doesn't have his act together. Even worse if it's made out of a household item like a plastic bear-shaped honey bottle. Then you're not just a stoner... you're a broke-ass stoner. P.S.: The bong water that has soaked into your carpet is starting to mildew.

262. OVERLY FAMILIAR WITH WAIT STAFF

This is an embarrassing attempt to show what a great guy you are. Acting like you're best friends with the waitress ("Hey, Susie, can you top me off here?"), calling the bartender "bro"...What you need to know here is everyone thinks you're an ass and is only speaking to you in the hope that you'll continue your Mr. Wonderful routine and leave a massive tip.

263. SHARE YOUR WORK STRESS ON A DATE

Whoooooh! We're having some fun now. What's next, details about your ulcer?

264. OWN NUNCHUCKS

Two possible scenarios here: You inhabit a paneled room in your parents' basement where you can be found practicing pretend karate moves in your underwear. Ick. Or you really use these to hurt people, in which case we'll just let ourselves out.

 265. *BICEP IMPLANTS/CALF IMPLANTS* Yes, this really is a procedure, and not a very normal-looking one. We have now entered the realm of the legitimately insane. Not only should you not be allowed to date, you should be neutered. With pliers.

 266. *PENIS ENLARGEMENT PILLS OR EQUIPMENT* We can get over the fact that you have a small penis. We can't get over the fact that you have a small brain. How can you actually believe this works? (It might work for like nine seconds, and hopefully you know that isn't nearly enough time.)

 267. *BAD TABLE MANNERS* Holding your fork like a tennis racket, tearing into your dinner before your date gets her food, eating with your mouth open, not putting your napkin in your lap. You are what's known as a cretin.

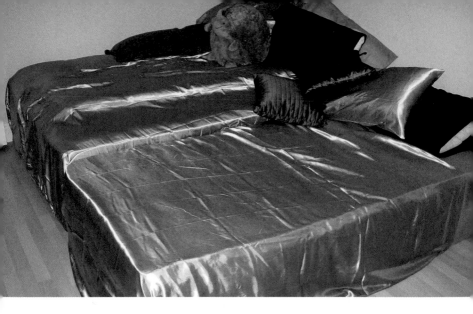

 268. REALLY WRONG SHEETS Satin, pilled, polyester, maroon, or themed bedding. All nasty, depressing, and uncomfortable. Even if you're kind of cute, no woman is crawling into that bed. Plus, when the house is on fire and you have to make a rope out of sheets to escape through the window, the firemen will totally make fun of your Power Ranger sheets. The only way to go here is white, 100 percent cotton with a thread count of no less than two hundred.

269. SCREAM LIKE A GIRL High-pitched screaming, in either excitement or fear, is of grave concern.

270. REV CAR AT STOP SIGNS We've checked our research and never in the history of dating has revving an engine gotten a guy a date. Is this supposed to be macho? What's next, burning rubber and peeling out? This is so ridiculous it's actually funny.

271. OWN A REPTILE Again, not getting it. It's not like it's cute or you can play with it. All it does is stare at people and make them want to leave. Also, the thought of your hands sifting through those pee-stained rocks when you clean the aquarium and then trying to touch us...no thank you.

272. USE A CURLING IRON OR FLAT IRON These are to be used by hairdressers and women, on women. If you find yourself looking in the mirror "creating loose waves" or making your hair "stick straight," you need to take some time and reevaluate...your gender.

*273. **SING SERIOUSLY*** Oh no…please stop unless you have a record deal. And even then, we'd rather just listen to the CD. A face-to-face, live performance gives us no choice but to flee.

 *274. **SELL BLOOD FOR MONEY*** You have pretty much hit rock bottom, as this is often the last resort after ransacking your couch for change or spending four hours rolling up a thousand pennies. You are years away from even thinking about dating a woman.

*275. **WINE IN A BOX*** No one expects you to be a wine expert. We don't even care what it is…it just has to be in a bottle. If you and your date end up getting married, you can buy all the boxed wine you like. For now, go with the glass.

 *276. **CROTCH-GRAB*** A true classic. Typically this happens after 1:00 A.M. and is accompanied by an aggressive shout-out of "Suck my dick." Lovely.

*277. **STEROIDS*** Juicing? Roiding? Not dating.

> *TRUE STORY: "At a Major League Baseball game, three obviously 'roided-out men made their way to their seats in the middle of the section. By the time they sat down, there were audible choruses of 'STEEEERRRRROOOOIIIIDS' heard from other fans. Everyone thinks these clowns are a joke." —Bill C., 29*

278. STACKS OF READING MATERIAL NEXT TO TOILET Too much reality. Any mystique you may have possessed has left the building. While we're at it, let's make a deal: We'll operate under the assumption that our bodies produce no embarrassing odors, sounds, or worse, and we'll do the same for you. Happily ever after.

279. NO PLAN FOR DATE There are nine words you should never, ever say to a woman you have any hopes of seeing again. Ready? Here they are…"I don't know…what do you feel like doing?" TAKE CHARGE.

280. ARM-WRESTLE IN PUBLIC Damn, did we miss the Stump Throw? Maybe after you're done, you could crush a beer can on your head. That's a TOTAL turn-on. Really.

281. FREQUENT THE SHOOTING RANGE The gun thing isn't working for us. If you're the kind of guy who likes to go and blow the heads off paper targets, we're going to go with incompatible.

282. PLAY VIDEO GAMES Unless you're a father playing the Wii with your son, fork over the remote. And if you play against your friends in tournaments and find yourself wearing a headset like you're working in a fast-food drive-thru, you may want to pause and go look at yourself in the mirror.

283. TALK ABOUT PLAYING VIDEO GAMES
Seriously, the best dinner conversation you can come up with is that you finally won the Sword of Incredible from Lord Darkmoor—and it took you only six hours? Of your life? Check, please.

284. JUVENILE HAND SIGNALS The most common being the thumbs-up, the gangsta throw-down, and the peace sign. There's nothing worse than a guy who needs to adopt trendy clichéd mannerisms that have nothing to do with him in an attempt to seem cool. What are you doing?

285. TWIRL YOUR MUSTACHE And if you have a mustache that's long enough to twirl, shouldn't you be tying a damsel to the train tracks somewhere or lifting twenties-era weights in a leopard-print unitard?

286. SCREAM AT REF OR PLAYERS At home or at a game. We recently saw a guy rant, "You suck, Kobe!" over and over again, red-faced and in danger of blowing a major blood vessel. Booing, swearing, taunting...all bad. And like you could do any better? We get that sports bring out emotion, but keep it together and have some civility.

You are allowed one (and only one) overly loud comment per game. And it better be entertaining to those around you—no one wants to hear "You suck, Kobe!" for two hours straight.

287. *NERVOUS WRECK WHILE TRAVELING*

Screaming at the cabdriver on the way to the airport, arriving four hours early, constantly thinking you've lost your ticket, elbowing people out of your way as you speed-walk to the gate...all grating and embarrassing. And you're like this every time you travel. Fun.

288. *OPEN-MOUTH BREATHING* This is another habit that guys have no idea they're doing. It's usually coupled with a blank, zombie-like stare, which makes us wonder if you've possibly had your brain sucked out of your ear.

289. *NOT OWNING A TV* If you can't afford a TV, that's fine. If you're walking around parties making sure that everyone knows you're too intelligent to bother watching television, you're an annoying weirdo. Guess what? We like talking about *The Office*. Everyone does.

290. *GROW POT ON WINDOWSILL* Are you really going to plant it, grow it, pick it, dry it, bake it, crumble it, roll it, and smoke it? That sounds like a ton of work for a four-minute buzz. By the way, last time we checked, possession of marijuana is still illegal in the United States.

291. *CARRY PURELL* "Hey, before we eat, want a dab of Purell?" If you're carrying Purell around in your pocket, you might want to reevaluate where and with whom you are hanging out. Also, constantly Purelling yourself around friends is not exactly a compliment.

292. *NO SENSE OF PERSONAL SPACE* Unless we're having sex, there is really no need for you to be two inches away while having a conversation. Back it up and back it off.

Mega Douche

The latest unexplainable phenomenon in terms of male stereotypes is a fantastically self-absorbed creature known as Mega Douche. In general terms, a Mega Douche is sort of what Rocky Balboa would look like midway through his sexual reassignment surgeries. Overly buffed, and wearing a ridiculously tight wife beater or Ed Hardy–esque T-shirt, multiple gold chains, bling, and a backward baseball cap, the Mega Douche is, unfortunately, just getting started. Where the Mega Douche really starts to define his "macho man in drag" quality is in his passionate adherence to female grooming habits. For roughly three hours, the MD is busy styling his overgelled hair into a "cactus" hairdo, self-tanning, plucking his eyebrows, and applying full makeup consisting of bronzer, eyeliner, mascara, and lipstick. Finishing off his look with a pair of diamond stud earrings, the Mega Douche has finally achieved the elevated and euphoric state known as "Scrotitude." Pulling himself away from his makeup table and free weights, Mega Douche is now ready to do what a Mega Douche does best...clubbing and "pulling some ass." Because he knows he is "the shit" and is impatient to show off his six-pack abs (real or painted on), the Mega Douche is shirtless within seven minutes of entering the club. He begins a frenzied display of ab flexing and fist pumping, which shockingly enough does often score him a few Hotts (hot chicks). Since Mega Douche is ready to "tap that ass," he and his Hott jump into his Corvette and head back to his place (also known as his parents' basement). After "banging his bitch," the Mega Douche slowly drifts off to sleep, smiling and self-satisfied after yet another day of magnificent Mega Douchery. But really...was there ever any doubt?

⚔ 293. WIMPY DRINKER

A.K.A. "Two Beer Bob." The worst. After two drinks you're wasted, and we end up pouring you into a cab by 9:00 P.M. You don't need a girlfriend. You need an infusion of male hormones. Today.

294. MANOREXIC Ordering salads for dinner, talking about carbs, asking if your jeans make your ass look big. Men are supposed to lose weight by exercising, not by acting like a woman.

 295. TAKE A DATE TO HOOTERS (AND RAVE ABOUT THE FOOD) You are either a classless pig or have a double-digit IQ. Or both. Even worse, we can tell the waitresses feel sorry for us because we're there with you.

 296. TEXT, E-MAIL, OR TAKE PERSONAL CALLS ON A DATE What this says to a girl is "I don't give a rat's ass about you. I'm not interested in you, your family, your work, or your friends." Actually, we love it when you step outside to talk to the "Commissioner" of your fantasy football league. It gives a nice guy the opportunity to come chat us up.

 297. FAIL TO WALK DATE TO CAR OR DOOR Yeah, tonight was fun, except for this next part, where I get bludgeoned with a tire iron by a random lunatic and left for dead. Thanks for nothing, d**khead.

298. NOT OWNING A CELL PHONE How is this possible?

> *TRUE STORY: Actually, we have a friend whose boyfriend didn't own a cell phone. He finally "broke down" and got one, but told her if she wanted to call he'd only have it on between 7:00 and 9:00 P.M. What the f***?*

299. BURP LOUDLY AND PROUDLY Maybe this was funny in third grade. Not funny now. Are you still using the word "butthole," too? And NEVER ask us to pull your finger.

 300. TACKY TEXTING Apparently, it's all the rage to ask a girl out via text. This is just lame and low-end. If you really cared, you'd call or ask her out in person. Secret tip: Any girl worth dating will completely ignore your lazy and rude digital transmissions.

 301. CHEW TOBACCO Your breath smells like a frog crawled under your tongue and died.

 302. TALK ABOUT HOW HOT YOUR EX/THE WAITRESS/MEGAN FOX IS How are we supposed to respond to this? Perhaps "Yes, she is hot," or maybe "Boy, if I were a man I would totally want to bang her." There's really nowhere to go after these types of comments.

 303. TALK ABOUT HOW EX WAS A "CRAZY BITCH" Of course she was. And you were ABSOLUTELY WONDERFUL.

> *Everyone is crazy. You just have to find the kind of crazy you're compatible with. There's even a word for this and everything: It's called "dating."*

☠ **304. *RIDE A CONTRAPTION*** What's with the bike that's eight feet high? How much attention do you need? This feels like another cry for help. Or riding a Segway. Are you serious? If your intent is to make everyone wonder what the hell you're doing as you go from point A to point B, then this is your vehicle.

305. DOESN'T HAVE E-MAIL Doesn't have date.

 306. REFER TO CELEBRITIES BY THEIR FIRST NAMES You don't know these people, so please stop referring to Robert De Niro and Martin Scorsese as "Bobby and Marty" while you are discussing their movies. "Leo," "Justin," "Ben and Matt"… seriously, enough. The guy who does this usually has *nothing* to do with the entertainment industry.

 ***307. "NOT FEELING WELL" AND WHINING ABOUT IT*** You have revealed yourself as a complete wuss. For all our talk about equal rights, no woman wants to date a wuss.

308. BERATE THE WAITSTAFF Nothing says "I am a complete and total prick" faster than a guy who is mean to the waitstaff. This is excusable only if you are simultaneously passing a kidney stone.

 309. ORDER WINE AT SPORTING EVENT Wow, such a great idea! We've heard Lambeau Field has an excellent wine cellar. Honestly, it's not even cool for a woman to order wine at a game. Live sporting events = cold beer.

310. CLEAN TEETH WITH RANDOM OBJECTS This habit is hard to break because it almost seems like a subconscious action. You're thinking about something else, and you unknowingly start cleaning your teeth with forks, paper clips, business cards, straws, whatever's handy. This may take care of the poppy seed that's been lodged in there since breakfast, but it does not increase your appeal.

311. OVERLY NUDE. You're the guy who could move into a nudist colony and not miss a beat. Sitting bare-assed on the couch, cooking breakfast with your "Johnson" flapping in the wind…really awkward and uncomfortable.

 Mostly nude would be better. Throw on a pair of boxer shorts and we're good. And make sure to close the bathroom door. We like a little mystery.

WHY YOUR GUY FRIENDS FIND YOU UNDATEABLE

100% RIDER

This next part is fascinating. Who knew you men were walking the planet in a silent rage, wrestling with your own list of Undateables? All this time we thought you were oblivious to things like other men's odd workout habits and ridiculous undergarments. But here you go. Single men...read up on why your guy friends never get around to setting you up with their sister, co-worker, girlfriend's friends, et cetera...

SAYING "WE'RE PREGNANT" One of the coolest guys we know said it best: "We 'Johnson-sporters' must police our own. The guy who says this is a tool. And reporting that 'We're TRYING to get pregnant' is a visual we can live without."
Jon S., 38, television executive

DRINKING COFFEE THROUGH A STRAW "No guy can look like a guy doing this. If you're in the hospital and can't move your arms, or just had dental work, we'll forgive you." *Peter K., 41, financial adviser*

JOGGING IN PLACE AT A STOPLIGHT "We get it; you're *really* taking this seriously. If you stop now, will you actually collapse? You look like a doofus."
Seth M., 36, liquidator

WEARING BIKINI UNDERWEAR "And when it's leopard print or mesh, it's even more f***ed up."
Roger B., 39, business owner

WRAPPING TOWEL AROUND HEAD "TURBAN-STYLE" AFTER SHOWER "Wrapping the towel is a full-fledged admission that you wish you didn't have a dick." *Seth M., 36, liquidator*

SHORTENING WORDS FOR NO REASON "Like, 'vacay' instead of 'vacation,' 'med rare' instead of 'medium rare' (yes, it happened), or 'cab' instead of 'cabernet.'" *Eric S., 50, psychoanalyst*

SPRAYING CROTCH WITH COLOGNE IN THE LOCKER ROOM "Getting dressed in the locker room is a world unto itself that no woman ever really wants to see. The guy that does this is a freak." *Art B., 35, mortgage broker*

LETTING A WOMAN WALK INTO A DARK HOUSE FIRST "Same guy who's afraid of bugs, runs like a girl, and drives slow in the left lane."
Scott C., 27, mortgage broker

GUYS WEARING HARLEY GEAR THAT DON'T RIDE A MOTORCYCLE "Sorry-ass, wannabe, poser." *William C., 27, banker*

HAVING A LIMP HANDSHAKE "Says it all. And kind of makes you want to break his hand." *Jorge I., 40, marketing executive*

DRIVING A HUMMER "The ultimate scrote. Wouldn't let my sister get in one. Dude must be way too into himself; maybe he's making up for something 'small.'" *Jon B., 23, grad student*

LETTING THE GIRL DRIVE ON THE FIRST DATE "Punk, here's a tip—the only exception is if you just had surgery." *Mike C., 37, entertainment industry*

OVER-IRONING Adam says this is the worst. "A rumpled cotton shirt is much more chic." *Adam G., 37, creative director* P.S.: Adam is the best-dressed man we know.

BEING TECHNOLOGICALLY CHALLENGED "Women want a guy who can do stuff, not a wimp." *Howie S., 34, insurance salesman*

USING THE PHRASE "THAT'S WHAT I'M TALKING ABOUT" "I don't understand what this even means. It just randomly comes out of guys' mouths in reference to ABSOLUTELY NOTHING." *Eric S., 50, psychoanalyst*

ALWAYS WANTING TO GO HOME EARLY "Must be a real fun guy. I double-dated with this whiner who kept looking at his watch and complaining about the time. His date, who was extremely hot, said, 'So sorry we're keeping you up.' Secretly, I think he had to get home to call his mommy." *A. J., 39, golf pro*

THE "NUDE STRETCHER" "There's this guy at the health club who just strips down and then does stretching exercises on the bench in the locker room for hours." *Dave H., 45, creative director*

HANGING IN STARBUCKS PRETENDING TO "WORK" "I call them Starbucks squatters. What's the deal with these dudes? We know jobs are tough to find these days, but then why are you spending four bucks on a latte? By hour two, you aren't fooling anyone." *Seth M., 36, liquidator*

SAYING "YO" TO A GIRL "It only worked for Rocky. And barely." *Alex P., 34, coach*

SAYING YOU CAN FIX SOMETHING AND THEN MAKING IT TEN TIMES WORSE "Break out the manual, brother, or spend the cash to call a professional; it's better to admit it than act like a know-it-all who actually knows nothing. Hope you don't get a flat tire on a date." *Lucas M., 43, medical transcriber*

OWNING A SIDEKICK IF OVER THIRTY "Okay, Paris Hilton. Make sure to put me in your fave five." *Nick K., 38, doctor*

NOT BEING ABLE TO THROW A BALL "Dude, if you aren't a jock, fine—but at least be able to throw a ball. And not wussy tossing. Someday there will be a barbecue, a company picnic, or the boys just wanting to toss around a baseball or a football. You don't have to be Derek Jeter or Tom Brady, just learn how to throw." *Cam M., 37, TV producer*

HAVING 'FRO HAIR ON CHEST COMING OUT OF SHIRT "Button up, dude. It's gross." *Scott M., 39, furniture fabricator*

NOT BEING ABLE TO TIE A TIE "I see these guys who get their tie tied at the store, then loosen it like a noose, put it back on, and tighten it up. Lame." *Paul U., 31, broker*

MEN IN HEAD-TO-TOE TRACKSUITS "See Turtle on *Entourage*. Especially suspect in all velour." *Andrew F., 31, lawyer*

DOING A PHANTOM GOLF SWING WHEN IN RANDOM CONVERSATION WITH A GROUP OF GUYS "Total f**khead. Tiger Woods is the only guy who is allowed to do this. Period." *Paul U., 31, broker*

OWNING A ROUND BRUSH "Before this year, I couldn't imagine any scenario where a guy would hold a blow dryer using a round brush to get his hairstyle just so...but my roommate had one. He also used bronzer, mousse, gel, and too much cologne. After a semester of his egomaniacal grooming habits, I took him out for a friendly game of touch football and tried to rip his head off." *Isaac K., 20, student*

THINKING DAVE & BUSTER'S IS A GOOD TIME "Bro, you've got no game. You're going to win her one of those prizes that really cost a dollar but you end up spending fifty. For date two...Chuck E. Cheese?" *Craig M., 33, account executive*

HONKING YOUR HORN AS A MEANS OF PICKING UP YOUR DATE "If anyone ever did this to my daughter, I'd blow his head off." *Sam G., 50, art director*

WEARING ATHLETIC SWEATBANDS WHEN NOT EXERCISING "Pretty much a loser. If you want to wear a bracelet, then get a watch." *Andy C., 28, trainer*

LISTENING TO MICHAEL BUBLÉ "Yeah, good plan. Blast that music on a date and you're sure to come off like a real stud." *Mark C., 36, agent*

BEING KNOWN AS "THE PORN GUY" AMONG GUY FRIENDS "Nobody's going out on a limb and setting this guy up." *Lucas M., 44, medical transcriber*

NOT BEING ABLE TO USE CHOPSTICKS "It's beyond wimpy to ask for a fork." *C. M., 27, lawyer*

ACTING SQUEAMISH ABOUT BAITING A HOOK "Grow a pair." *Doug L., 32, editor*

CONCLUSION

While creating this book, we had no intention of writing a conclusion, figuring we had said QUITE ENOUGH already. But as we were finishing the final chapter, we received a photo of one of our featured "Undateables" who had since transformed himself into someone completely "Dateable," and now even has the hot wife to prove it. (For the Undateable version of Jeff Murray, go to page 14. Yes, it's true.)

Along with this picture of his new and improved self, he had this to say: "I included a picture of my wife and me to prove that even the 'Undateable' can still have hope. Thanks for the opportunity to laugh at myself."

And so with that we say to you: Lose the nasty flavor saver and go pull some ass.

Actually, no. What we really want to say is this: You're probably a pretty nice guy, and after an unspecified number of alterations, you too can become Dateable.

And remember, SWAGGER and CONFIDENCE can almost always counteract the damage caused by a really bad pair of Dad Jeans...

Ellen Anne

Ellen Rakieten is currently President of Ellen Rakieten Entertainment. For over twenty-three years she was a key force in creating, developing, writing, and producing *The Oprah Winfrey Show*, helping to make it one of the most successful television shows in history. She has also launched and promoted hundreds of bestselling products, books, movies, and careers. Her razor-sharp instincts on "what sells" make her one of the most highly acclaimed and sought-after executive producers in the entertainment industry.

Anne Coyle has worked as a senior advertising copywriter; her work in print, radio, and television won high honors in numerous national and international award shows. She is currently president and owner of Anne Coyle Interiors, a nationally acclaimed interior design firm. Her design work appears regularly in many shelter publications, including *O at Home*, *Metropolitan Home*, and *Elle Decor*.